"In a time where both too wild and too mild spiritualities abound, it is audacious to put forward a book on liturgical mysticism. It is a category which comprises the broad and deep mystical core of sacramental liturgy, as well as the indispensability of liturgy in Christian mysticism. Attitudes of indifference, resistance, and even sheer ignorance are to be expected, for it is by no means evident to prophetically remind Christians of the essentials of their faith. Yet here is why Fagerberg's newest book is as important as it is needed. First, it offers opportunity for personal reflections about where one stands in the tension between creation and redemption. Second, it draws upon a refined and clever selection of sources, many of which are absolutely worth (re)reading, ruminating upon, and digesting. And third, it continues to enrich liturgical theology by amplifying its horizon and solidifying the foundation on which it rests. I have not a single doubt that this book will be a milestone in the rediscovery of the liturgy's centrality for Christian living in today's world, but also that it will agitate people, both in the sense of irritating and stimulating. And that is why it should be thoroughly studied and discussed widely."

JORIS GELDHOF
Katholieke Universiteit Leuven

"What David Fagerberg has done is author a work that articulates the beauty of God's own self gift in Christ. In so doing, he has authored a short course on Catholicism itself. This 'course' is not academic in a narrow intellectualist sense. Rather, his words move the whole person to desire worship and the life that is given therein, holiness. His prose elicits prayer and wonder and thus silence and contemplation. Approaching life as centered within the Eucharistic Liturgy we become mystics bearing within us Christ's own self-donative gift to the poor. As Fagerberg's thought continues to mature, using both 'lungs' of the Church, East and West, our debt to him grows. We can only hope he continues to generously share with us the fruit of his own prayer."

DEACON JAMES KEATING
*Institute for Priestly Formation
Creighton University*

"For over three decades, David Fagerberg has given us a comprehensive vision of the liturgy as the fundamental milieu of Christian faith and life. The liturgy is not just one more thing Christians 'do': the way Christians think, act, and even feel—in short, everything Christians are and do—is formed by the Church's worship. In *Liturgical Mysticism*, Fagerberg continues his articulation of how the Mystery is embodied and lived by those who partake in the Church's sacramental worship, which is itself a participation in the eternal 'liturgy' of Father, Son, and Holy Spirit. Believers can be assured that their sacramental worship of God is indeed mystical, insofar as it configures them according to *the* Mystery, and liberates them from the constraints of a mysticism defined in the narrow terms of reflexive self-consciousness."

MSGR. MICHAEL HEINTZ
Mount St. Mary's Seminary

"David Fagerberg is establishing a unique voice. The language and the vivid images he develops are his response to being deeply stunned by the liturgy and all that happens in its celebration. He is seeking to claim mystical life for ordinary Christians, by which he means the Paschal Mystery, through the liturgy, taking up its home deeply within us and becoming the substance of our lives."

ABBOT JEREMY DRISCOLL, O.S.B.
Mount Angel Abbey

LITURGICAL
MYSTICISM

LITURGICAL
MYSTICISM

DAVID W. FAGERBERG

EMMAUS
ACADEMIC

Steubenville, Ohio
www.emmausacademic.com

EMMAUS
A C A D E M I C

Steubenville, Ohio
www.emmausacademic.com
A Division of The St. Paul Center for Biblical Theology
Editor-in-Chief: Scott Hahn
1468 Parkview Circle
Steubenville, Ohio 43952

Library of Congress Cataloging-in-Publication Data
Names: Fagerberg, David W., 1952- author.
Title: Liturgical mysticism / David W. Fagerberg.
Description: Steubenville : Emmaus Academic, 2019.
Identifiers: LCCN 2019017681 | ISBN 9781949013672 (hard cover) | ISBN
    9781949013689 (pbk.)
Subjects: LCSH: Mysticism--Catholic Church. | Catholic Church--Liturgy.
Classification: LCC BV5082.3 .F34 2019 | DDC 248.2/2--dc23
LC record available at https://lccn.loc.gov/2019017681

Cover design and layout by Emily Demary
Cover Image: *Mass Said by the Canon de La Porte on the High Altar of Notre Dame de Paris* (1708–10) by Jean Jouvenet, The Musee du Louvre, Paris

Nihil Obstat: Msgr. Michael Heintz
Censor Librorum
February 10, 2019

Imprimatur: Kevin C. Rhoades
Bishop of Fort Wayne - South Bend
February 18, 2019

For my parents, and Elizabeth's, who are now all experiencing the mystery firsthand.

TABLE OF CONTENTS

Prologue

ALTHOUGH THIS APPEARS FIRST, it was written last. It is a sketch, for the reader's benefit, of a finish line I know now but did not know when I started writing. I wanted to connect liturgy and mysticism in some way and for some reason—it seemed intuitively proper—but I did not know how or why. I knew what paths I would not be following. It would not be a history of mysticism as expressed by individuals or various schools, nor a description of mysticism at the psychological level, nor a doctrinal treatment of theological themes like the gifts of the Holy Spirit. These kind of treatments can be easily found by the reader elsewhere. I, rather, wanted to propose a unity between mysticism and the three topics that have so far occupied me, namely, liturgy, theology, and asceticism. I supposed that there was an intrinsic unity here, but did not know how to picture it when I began.[1] The most significant work was done for the Archbishop Dwyer Lectures at Mount Angel Seminary (chapters 2, 4, and 6); eschatology stood in the background of my thinking, like a giant, and was addressed in a paper for the Academy for Catholic Theology (chapter 7); and from the classroom I had in mind to apply another feature of liturgy

---

[1] Since publishing *On Liturgical Asceticism*, which used almost exclusively Eastern Christian authors, I purposely began reading in Western Christian spirituality. Besides revisiting classic spiritual authors (John of the Cross, Teresa of Avila, Bonaventure, Ignatius, the French School of Jean Berulle, Francis de Sales, and François Fénelon), I found some recent authors helping my understanding: John Arintero, Barthelemy Froget, Jean Grou, Louis Lallemant, Anselm Stolz, Divo Barsotti, Reginald Garrigou-Lagrange, Auguste Saudreau, Francis Libermann, and Jordan Auman.

(chapter 1), the foundational place of baptism (chapter 3), and the role of faith, hope, and love when it comes to our personal participation in Christ's cross and resurrection (chapter 5).

It would have been easy to say the liturgist is a mystic, and the mystic is a liturgist, and leave it at that: two dimensions of the Christian life placed side-by-side, each exerting a mutual influence on the other. The simple way out would have been to nudge the two closer together, searching first for mystical dimensions in liturgical texts and practices, and then for liturgical consequences or expressions in mystical experiences. But I was predisposed to approach liturgical mysticism as I had approached liturgical theology, and in this understanding, liturgy is foundational to theology, so I supposed that might be the same for mysticism, even though I did not know exactly how this would work. I had been led by two mentors to think of liturgy as the substance (*sub-stantia*) of Christian theology and spirituality, Alexander Schmemann and Aidan Kavanagh.

Schmemann's impact on liturgical studies has been his proposal that liturgy is the source of, not just an object for, theology. He writes, "The *leitourgia*—being the unique expression of the Church, of its faith and of its life—must become the basic source of theological thinking."[2] Because liturgical theology is the theology conducted by the Church in her liturgical life, the *lex orandi* we experience in liturgy is the ontological condition of theology.

> The formula *lex orandi est lex credendi* means nothing else than that theology is *possible* only within the Church, i.e. as a fruit of this new life in Christ, granted in the sacramental *leitourgia*, as a witness to the eschatological fullness of the Church, as in other terms, a participation in this *leitourgia*. The problem of the relationship between liturgy and theology is not for the Fathers a problem of priority or authority. Liturgical tradition is not an "authority" or a *locus theologicus*; it is the ontological condition of theology, of the proper understanding of kerygma, of the Word of God, because it is in the Church, of which the *leitourgia* is the expression and the life, that the sources of theology are functioning as precisely "sources."[3]

---

[2]   Alexander Schmemann, "Theology and Liturgical Tradition," in *Liturgy and Tradition*, ed. Thomas Fisch (Crestwood, NY: St. Vladimir's Seminary Press, 1990), 11–12.

[3]   Schmemann, "Theology and Liturgical Tradition," 18.

Kavanagh further refined the thought by referring to this as "primary theology" and identifying who does it. "The true primary theologian in the Church is the liturgical assembly in each and every one of its members."[4] The community encounters God, undergoes an adjustment, and this adjustment "is theology being born, theology in the first instance. It is what tradition has called *theologia prima*."[5] Kavanagh thought we could only understand this if we took a certain verb seriously, even if it is often omitted in casual quotation.

> That verb was *statuat*, as in *lex supplicandi legem statuat credendi*: The law of worshiping founds the law of believing. So long, I think, as the verb stays in the sentence it is not possible to reverse subject and predicate any more than one can reverse the members of the statement: the foundation supports the house. . . . The old maxim means what it says.[6]

Both of these men presented an approach to liturgy that seemed different to me from the way liturgy was approached by much of the academy. In most approaches, the academy treated liturgy as either a subject matter for investigation (biblical theology talks about the Bible, moral theology talks about ethical questions, and liturgical theology talks about vestments and rubrics) or a method for approaching other topics (historical theology treats the historical development of doctrine, narrative theology starts with stories instead of propositions, and liturgical theology explores a doctrine's spiritual consequences). In other words, scholarship had connected liturgy with theology in only two ways: either do theology upon liturgical phenomena, or make liturgy into a special approach to theology. It began to seem to me that in order to bear the interpretation that Schmemann and Kavanagh had proposed, the concept of liturgy being used was too thin. We had been trying to simply mix some liturgy into academic theology, like mixing some oil into water, when the real goal should be defining the deep reality named by the conjoined words. The public, ceremonial cult was only like the part of the liturgical iceberg that we can see. What is underneath it? To answer this, I distinguished *leitourgia* from liturgy, first in my

---

[4] Aidan Kavanagh, *On Liturgical Theology* (New York: Pueblo, 1984), 150.
[5] Kavanagh, *On Liturgical Theology*, 74.
[6] Kavanagh, *On Liturgical Theology*, 91.

dissertation and then in a revised second edition of its publication.[7]

But there was more. Judging from the challenges faced in explaining this notion of liturgical theology, it seemed that the second term needed to be thickened as well. Not only did liturgy need to become *leitourgia* but theology needed to become *theologia*. Without that, theology occurred only in the academy and calling liturgy "primary theology" was really only saying that liturgy provided straw for an academic Rumpelstiltskin to spin into real theological gold. Schmemann and Kavanagh were claiming that primary theology is done in the liturgical matrix itself. I found my thicker definition by turning to the ascetical tradition in Eastern Christianity.[8] Evagrius of Pontus identifies three steps in disciplining (*askesis*) our mind and will to conform to Christ: he calls the first stage of battling the passions *praktike*, he calls the second stage of contemplating creation's revelation of its Creator *physike*, and he calls the final stage of union with God *theologia*. The path of asceticism ends up in an experiential knowledge of the Trinity, an experiential state that no one said is restricted to monks alone. Theology is pneumatic communion with *Theos* through the *Logos*, and every Christian is taken up by the Holy Spirit through their baptism into this dynamic. Asceticism may have been perfected in the sands of the desert, but it originates in the waters of the font, and for me this connected asceticism to liturgy. And it depends upon a definition of theology that does not begin in the card catalogue but begins with fasting and almsgiving. Liturgy and asceticism were not to be placed side-by-side, a division of labor between ecclesiastics and monastics, any more than liturgy and theology were to be left side-by-side, a division of labor between Church and academy. If liturgy meant sharing the life of Christ (being washed in his resurrection, eating his body), and if askesis meant discipline (in the sense of forming), then liturgical asceticism could be defined as the discipline required to become an icon of Christ and make his image visible in our faces. Theologia was knowing the Trinity, but in the biblical sense of "knowing." I arrived, therefore, at this definition of liturgy: *Liturgy is the perichoresis of the Trinity kenotically extended to invite our synergistic ascent into deification.*

---

[7] David Fagerberg, *Theologia Prima: What Is Liturgical Theology?* (Chicago: Hillenbrand Books, 2004).

[8] David Fagerberg, *On Liturgical Asceticism* (Washington, DC: Catholic University of America Press, 2013).

Well, if liturgy did not stand in an artificial conjunction with
theology, and if liturgy did not stand in an artificial conjunction with
asceticism, then shouldn't liturgy have more than an artificial conjunction with mysticism? If liturgical theology understood liturgy
itself to be theological activity, then shouldn't liturgical mysticism
understand liturgy itself to be mystical activity? And although I had
not yet thought consciously about mysticism, was there not already
a dimension of mysticism in liturgical asceticism since the objective
of asceticism is union with God? I should not, then, be satisfied with
looking for nuggets of mysticism in the liturgy, or for liturgical icing
on mystical experiences. Liturgy + theology = the Church's *lex orandi*
received as *theologia prima*. Liturgy + theology + asceticism = the subjective cost of union with God, a theologia that already has a mystical
flavor. If I had argued that Mrs. Murphy was a liturgical theologian,
though not of the academic kind; and if I had argued that Mrs. Murphy was a liturgical ascetic, though not of the monastic kind; might I
not also argue that Mrs. Murphy is a liturgical mystic, though not of
the extraordinary kind?

The mystical life is the normal crowning of the Christian life
because eternal life is the life for which we yearn, for which we are
disciplined, toward which we strive, for which we have eschatological hope, which we exercise in love, which inspires faith. Here is
that point made by four significant modern authors: John Arintero
states, "Even in its strictest significance or most characteristic state
the mystical life is undoubtedly nothing but the complete manifestation of the Christian life or, rather, the development of the graces
received in baptism."[9] Garrigou-Lagrange describes "the traditional
teaching, which is more and more accepted today: namely, that the
normal prelude of the vision of heaven, the infused contemplation
of the mysteries of faith, is, by docility to the Holy Ghost, prayer,
and the cross, accessible to all fervent interior souls."[10] Anselm Stolz
writes, "The believer does not merely see that the truth is of God
and that he ought to believe it"; rather, his belief "develops into an
experience of the divine truth. . . . At this stage, in the teaching of
the older theology, the simple believer becomes theologian, Gnostic,

---

[9] John Arintero, *The Mystical Evolution In the Development and Vitality of the Church*,
vol. 2 (Rockford, IL: Tan Books, 1978), 404.

[10] Reginald Garrigou-Lagrange, *The Three Ages of the Interior Life*, vol. 1 (London:
Catholic Weight, 2014), 2.

and mystic."[11] And Jordan Auman therefore says, "The mystical experience is not an extraordinary grace similar to charismatic graces but is the normal consequence of the operation of the gifts of the Holy Spirit. We have already implied this in the previous explanation, but it is well to emphasize the fact that mysticism is the flowering of the life of grace and the crowning achievement of the perfection of charity."[12] Certainly there are people with extraordinary graces alongside the ordinary mystic, like there are extraordinary saints alongside baptized Christians, like there are heroic ascetics in the desert to inspire ordinary Christians in the world, but mysticism is a normal crowning of the Christian life, and the Christian life is liturgical. Therefore, liturgical mysticism.

Mrs. Murphy, though an ascetic, is not the type of ascetic who has left the world. Her liturgical mysticism is mundane, practiced in daily life and in ordinary circumstances, alongside her liturgical theology and her liturgical asceticism. This I had already begun to explore[13] and it continues here. We sometimes assume that a choice must be made between Church and world, mystery and the mundane, eschaton and time, liturgy and life, but the choice is bogus and the assumption is false. The Constitution on the Sacred Liturgy says participation in the Paschal mystery can occur constantly, everywhere.

> For well-disposed members of the faithful, the liturgy of the sacraments and sacramentals sanctifies almost every event in their lives; they are given access to the stream of divine grace which flows from the paschal mystery of the passion, death, the resurrection of Christ, the font from which all sacraments and sacramentals draw their power. There is hardly any proper use of material things which cannot thus be directed toward the sanctification of men and the praise of God.[14]

Liturgical mysticism is the development of graces received in baptism; *liturgical asceticism* is the process which develops those graces; the

---

[11] Anselm Stolz, *The Doctrine of Spiritual Perfection* (New York: Crossroad, 2001), 175–176.

[12] Jordan Aumann, *Spiritual Theology* (New York: Bloomsbury Continuum, 2018), 127.

[13] David Fagerberg, *Consecrating the World* (New York: Angelico Press, 2016).

[14] Paul VI, Constitution on the Sacred Liturgy *Sacrosanctum Concilium* (December 4, 1963), §61.

product of those graces is a *liturgical theologian* who is enlightened. Liturgical mysticism wants to know what is done inside a person by the liturgy.

The two operational theaters of the liturgy are the Church and the soul, and the tradition has always treated them together. The bride in the Song of Solomon has always been understood to be both the Church and the soul, simultaneously. I am following suit when I propose that the liturgy is the power of God ("the perichoresis of the Trinity kenotically extended . . .") to impact both the Church and the individual soul (". . . to invite our synergistic ascent into deification"). In the Church, this power is visible and sacramental; in the soul it is invisible and mystical. I will call the former *sacramental liturgy* and the latter *liturgical mysticism*. The former is exterior liturgy, the latter is interior liturgy. If we think of an individual person as a cell in the body of the Church, then think of sacramental liturgy as corporeal and liturgical mysticism as cellular. The Church is the bride of Christ at both levels: sacramental liturgy is Christ entering his Church, and liturgical mysticism is the Church-at-liturgy entering the soul. Lambert Beauduin put the matter in syllogistic terms in the paper that is sometimes called the origin of the liturgical movement.

> The superabundant source of all supernatural life is the sacerdotal power of the High Priest of the New Covenant.
>
> But this sanctifying power Jesus Christ does not exercise here below except through the ministry of a *visible sacerdotal hierarchy.*
>
> Hence close union with this hierarchy in the exercise of its priesthood is for every Christian and Catholic soul the authentic mode of union with the priesthood of Jesus Christ, and consequently the primary and indispensable source of supernatural life.[15]

This source of life, this energy of love, this supernatural and sacred power has sustained the world as a divine liturgical economy since its creation; it took prophetic and typological form in Israel's prophets,

---

[15] Lambert Beauduin, *Liturgy: The Life of the Church* (Farnborough, UK: Saint Michael's Abbey, 2002), 13.

priests, and kings; it now has visible, sacerdotal, sacramental, fleshly form as the mystical body of Christ that is formed and fed by his Eucharistic body; and it still awaits its final consummation in the eschaton. But Jean Daniélou says it's all one and the same mystery.

> The Christian faith has only one object, the mystery of Christ dead and risen. But this unique mystery subsists under different modes: it is prefigured in the Old Testament, it is accomplished historically in the earthly life of Christ, it is contained in mystery in the sacraments, it is lived mystically in souls, it is accomplished socially in the Church, it is consummated eschatologically in the heavenly kingdom. [16]

This river of liturgy flows from the heavenly throne, pools up in the Church, and overflows its lip to flood our personal lives.

Liturgical theology asks, "What happens in liturgy?" Liturgical mysticism asks, "What happens *to us* in liturgy?" I could therefore possibly call liturgical mysticism "personal liturgy" if there was no danger of being misunderstood to mean private and exclusive and self-constructed—as in, "my personal liturgy." I could use the term if I were instead correctly understood to mean liturgy as it occurs on the level of person. Perhaps I should call it *hypostasized liturgy*. Hypostasis was the Greek term for person, and theologians were able to use it in Christology to affirm the union of two natures in one hypostasis, and the harmony of three hypostases in the one *ousia* of the Trinity. Its meaning can be seen in its component parts: *hypo* means under or beneath, and *stasis* means a position or standing. Hypostatic refers to that which "stands under" something, giving it actual existence and real being, evident in its translation into Latin as *sub-stantia*, substance. Hypostasis names the distinct member of some group that shares the same nature. Maximus the Confessor said, "An angel is distinct from another angel, a man from another man, an ox from another ox, a dog from another dog, by reason of their hypostasis, not their nature and essence."[17] Every dog has a canine nature, but this

---

[16] Jean Daniélou, "Le symbolism des rites baptismaux," *Dieu vivant*, quoted in Robert Taft, "Toward a Theology of the Christian Feast," *Beyond East and West* (Rome: Pontifical Oriental Institute, 1997), 29.

[17] Maximus the Confessor, quoted in Christoph Schönborn, *God's Human Face* (San Francisco: Ignatius Press, 1994), 104.

dog is not that dog. The Father and Son and Holy Spirit have the same divine nature or essence, but this person is not that person.

A nature or essence or being becomes personal when it hypostasizes. G. L. Prestige gives us a visual image of this from a primitive use of the word. The term hypostasis was applied to "the dregs of wine in the cask. There is nothing new in this usage, since Aristotle and Hippocrates are both quoted . . . as using the term to denote sediment. However, it also occurs in a wider sense to denote the underneath or hidden part of any object."[18] In a wine barrel, some sediment settles (*stasis*) at the bottom (*hypo*), and though most of the cask is liquid, winemakers still today speak of red wines "throwing sediment" when they age. In the human race, a nature is shared but it "settles" into a unique person.

I can use the word for my purposes, then. When the liturgy in the barrel hypostasizes, becomes personal, settles in an individual Christian life, it is hypostatic liturgy. The liturgical theologian is a liturgical ascetic who has been formed by the liturgy's *lex orandi* to become a liturgical mystic. Liturgy's business is to celebrate the Paschal mystery. It does so in a visible, historical, corporal, ecclesiastical, sacramental way, but that mystery also hypostasizes in us, descends to us, takes up its home in us, becomes the substance of our lives. Liturgical mysticism is when liturgy takes up residence in our lives. For this reason, the examination of mysticism as a dimension of liturgy has expanded my understanding of liturgy, but it has done so in a unitive way, not an additive way. This proved an intrinsic unity of liturgical-ascetical-mystical-theology in Christian *leitourgia* that I had not anticipated when I began. It presented itself to me over the course of my exploration, and the reader is welcome to join me through its twists and turns. Or, the reader might spare himself the trouble and be content with the definition I found at the end, recorded here at the beginning. *Liturgical mysticism is the Trinitarian mystery, mediated by sacramental liturgy and hypostasized as personal liturgy, to anchor the substance of our lives.*

Solemnity of Mary Mother of God
January 2019

---

[18] G. L. Prestige, *God in Patristic Thought* (London: SPCK, 1985), 163.

CHAPTER 1

AN ENTHRALLING LITURGY

WHY PUT THE MODIFIER "LITURGICAL" in front of the term "mysticism"? After all, many people think the two have gotten along fine without each other for years, maybe centuries. Like mother hens each sorting their own brood, people interested in liturgy gather things rubrical, canonical, ritualistic, sacramental, ceremonial, and pious, while people interested in mysticism gather things divine, ultimate, transcendent, allegorical, enigmatic, and otherworldly. The contrast appears on several fronts. Liturgy is habitual and formal, while mysticism is unexpected and uncontrollable; liturgy uses public rites, while mysticism involves private experience; liturgy is made up of sensible sacraments, while mysticism takes one beyond perceptual apprehension; liturgy is for ordinary people, while mysticism is for extraordinary saints. The two ideas might mutually repel, such as one feels when pressing together common ends of a magnet. Why bring the two within a hundred conceptual miles of each other?

Let me begin with a compendious list.

First one side: why call mysticism liturgical? Because mysticism is the Paschal mystery we liturgically celebrate coming to us; because mysticism is nursed at the breast of Mother Church; because it arises from the sacraments; because mysticism flows from the side of the crucified incarnate High Priest; because mysticism is exercised in the Church, the mystical body of Christ; because mysticism is a responsive sacrificial action made after one is stripped of self-love; because mysticism is the Church ascending into the luminous darkness that

1

beckons her; because mysticism is practiced in the place where our sin is drowned, namely, the empty tomb turned sideways and flooded; because mysticism depends upon a God's-eye view that was created when baptismal waters rinsed sin's chemical burn from our eyes, and the first thing we saw was Christ, waiting for us; because mysticism is nourished by a food given to us by the Son of Man (John 6:26) that endures to eternal life; because the exercise of mysticism requires theological virtues infused in us at baptism; because mysticism's practice is neither private nor particular nor idiosyncratic, but instead corporate and common and ecclesial; because mysticism is oriented to the deification required to enjoy heaven; because mysticism is a reawakened appetite for God; because mysticism is our liturgical eros; because mysticism is an experience already of the unification of earth and heaven; because liturgy reminds us that mysticism is normal. (These are the subject of the next chapter.)

Now the other side: why call liturgy mystical? Because liturgy enthralls; because the aim of liturgy is holiness and a mystic is a holy person; because in Middle English "mystic" meant to have symbolic meaning or interpretation, which the liturgy always does; because mysticism is union with God, a theologia that is the source and summit of liturgy; because mysticism is transformative contact with the mysteries of Christ, which is what liturgy celebrates; because mysticism is not private, but has an ecclesial dimension, and liturgy is not merely public, but also has an intensely personal dimension; because the liturgical person—the *homo adorans*—has no other end in view; because mysticism is a foretaste of heavenly liturgy; because liturgy is heaven's descension and mysticism is humanity's ascension; because liturgical catabasis induces mystical anabasis; because the mystical life is proper relationship to God, and proper relationship to God is worship, and worship is *logike latreia* (Rom 12:12). (These are the subject of this chapter.)

I want to present the liturgically formed ascetic, who has learned liturgical theology's *theologia prima*, as a liturgical mystic. Liturgical mysticism is grounded in the life of the Church, which is life in the new eon and reflected in a network of Church doctrines. Schmemann says, "[A]ll genuine theology is, of necessity and by definition, *mystical*. This means not that theology is at the mercy of individual and irrational 'visions' and 'experiences,' but that it is rooted in, made indeed *possible*, by the Church's experience of herself as *communion of the Holy Spirit.*"[1] Mysticism is not an element extrinsically added on to theology or piety, it is a quality intrinsic to all Christian life. Liturgical mysticism is the Church's experience of herself as communion of the Holy Spirit, and this eschatological experience involves both the death of the Old Adam (liturgical asceticism) and the joy and peace that make us partakers of the Kingdom here and now.

On the one hand, considering liturgists as mystics will extend liturgy into all the dimensions of our lives, and we should not overlook liturgy's mystical dimension even as we examine its history and rubrics and ritual performance. On the other hand, considering mystics as liturgists will ground the understanding of mysticism in the Church, and not in extraordinary personalities. Mysticism is ordinary for Christians insofar as Christians are a people of *leitourgia*. The potential for a mystical element in liturgy can be detected in the definition of liturgy I adopted even before considering liturgical mysticism. *Liturgy* is *the perichoresis of the Trinity kenotically extended to invite our synergistic ascent into deification.*[2] Couple that with John Tauler's claim that "the soul sees how the whole admirable mystery of the Trinity reechoes and is reproduced in the soul itself,"[3] and we will understand liturgical mysticism as the perichoresis of the Trinity (i.e., liturgy) echoing in us individually. The four elements in my definition each make room for this understanding.

First, perichoresis means going beyond one's place and making room for the other: it is the reciprocity and interpenetration by the Persons of the Trinity. The word was first used in Christology to describe the relationship of the two natures in the one person Jesus, and, having proven its value, the word came to be also used in Triadology when describing the relationship of the Persons of the Trinity. This concept of perichoresis can thus actually summarize all of Christian doctrine when it affirms (i) one person, two natures; (ii) three persons, one nature. Liturgy is the activity of the Trinity, and liturgical mysticism is a person's participation in that activity.

Second, this circulation of love overflows and kenotically exceeds itself, first in the creation of non-divine beings, and second in the re-

[1] Alexander Schmemann, "Freedom in the Church," in *Church, World, Mission* (Crestwood, NY: Saint Vladimir's Seminary Press, 1979), 188.
[2] David Fagerberg, *On Liturgical Asceticism* (Washington, DC: Catholic University of America Press, 2013), 9.
[3] Tauler, *Institutions*, ch. 28, quoted in Arintero, *The Mystical Evolution In the Development and Vitality of the Church*, vol. 2 (Rockford, IL: Tan Books, 1978), 359.

demption of lost members. Although it is more common to use *kenosis* about Christ's self-emptying in the Incarnation, it has also been used to describe the sort of "going outside himself" that the Creator does in creation. The perichoresis of the Trinity kenotically extends itself when God "relinquishes his utter transcendence in order to dwell in all things"[4] (Maximus the Confessor) and enters into the sort of communion that a lover has when he "is placed outside himself, and made to pass into the object of his love, inasmuch as he wills good to the beloved"[5] (Thomas Aquinas). The kenosis-act in this definition of liturgy refers to both creation and redemption, the big bang and Bethlehem. The liturgical reason for existence is to invite mystical communion of the creature with the Creator, and a liturgical cosmology will define the duty of man's place in it, which involves consecrating the world as cosmic priest.

Third, there is an ascent, though not one done automatically. *Auto-matos* means "self-acting, moving or acting on its own," and here we do nothing on our own. Yet although our ascent is graced, we must be willingly involved. Louis Bouyer writes,

> While no automatism is possible in mystical development any more than any infallible and necessarily effective technique, it can and must be said that no mystical life is ever anything other than the fully conscious but fully normal development of our personal apprehension of what the Word of God reveals to us of Christ in the Church, of what is given us therein through the sacraments: the gift of grace reveals to faith, working through charity.[6]

Our ascent is not mechanical, it is personal; it is not compulsory, it is voluntary. This co-involvement is called *synergia* in the Eastern tradition, which Lev Gillet defines as two powers equal in necessity but unequal in importance. "The incorporation of man into Christ and his union with God requires the co-operation of two unequal,

---

4   Maximus the Confessor, "Various Texts on Theology, the Divine Economy, and Virtue and Vice," in *The Philokalia*, vol. 2 (London: Faber and Faber, 1981), 281.

5   Thomas Aquinas, *Summa Theologiae*, trans. Fathers of the English Dominican Province, vol. 2 (Benziger Brothers, 1948; Westminster, MD: Christian Classics, 1981), I, q. 20, a. 2, resp. 1. Hereafter abbreviated as *ST*.

6   Louis Bouyer, *Introduction to Spirituality* (Collegeville, MN: Liturgical Press, 1961), 304.

but equally necessary, forces: divine grace and human will."[7] This can be expressed in Western scholastic and causal categories, too. Garrigou-Lagrange says, "One part does not come from us and the other from God. The act is entirely from God as from its first cause, and it is entirely from us as from its second cause."[8] Therefore, "the first cause does not render secondary causes superfluous."[9] The principal subject of the liturgy is the Holy Spirit, but we co-operate in the liturgy with him. God energizes, man synergizes. The kenotic descension does not force our mystical ascension, it makes it possible. The longing for God felt by the human race is not disappointed, but the gate through which we are invited to come to mystical union is narrow.

And fourth, all this leads to deification. This is itself a mystical doctrine. God became man so that man might become god—so said nearly all the Church Fathers. We are to become by grace what Christ is by nature; we become gracefully what he is naturally, and therein we see the result toward which incarnation works: God's descent raises. Although we often think of incarnation as Christ simply descending from a high place to a low place, the Creed attributed to Athanasius describes it as an assumption, as the "taking of the manhood into God" (*sed assumptione humanitatis in Deum*). The Son of God descended so that the sons of Adam could be lifted up; to his *kenosis* corresponds our *prokope*[10] (meaning furtherance, progress; from *pro-kopto*, meaning advancement by chopping down whatever impedes progress). By assuming flesh in the Incarnation he chopped down impediments of sin and death and Satan so we could advance, at last, toward our teleological end. The twin purposes of liturgy are the sanctification of man and the glorification of God, both of which come together in liturgical mysticism.

For liturgy to have this mystical dimension it must seize us, take us over, be arresting. Liturgy must make a dent in us. To even think this way, we must abandon our insipid view of liturgy as our construct, our emotional support, our self-gushing assertion. We facilely agree with this in principle but do not really know what it means. For

---

[7] Lev Gillet, *Orthodox Spirituality* (Crestwood: St. Vladimir's Seminary Press, 1987), 23.

[8] Reginald Garrigou-Lagrange, *The Three Ages of the Interior Life*, vol. 2 (London: Catholic Weight, 2014), 146.

[9] Garrigou-Lagrange, *The Three Ages of the Interior Life*, 2:307.

[10] Treated in chapter three of my *Consecrating the World* (New York: Angelico Press, 2016).

liturgy to be mystical, it cannot be egotistical. In order to conform us to God, liturgy must not conform to us but we to it, and that means liturgy has a formality that comes from being an *opus Dei*. We are resistant to liturgy's formality, says Paul Holmer, because "[w]e live in a day of informality. All kinds of domains evince lack of confidence in system, order, formality and tradition. . . . My overarching goal is to confront that vague notion that liturgy is in a bad way because it is formal."[11] The formality of liturgy is not just a matter of style, it is a matter of theologically agreeing that the form of liturgy is determined by the transcendent and unchanging God.

> It is not as if God is changing so rapidly that new material has to be inserted into the liturgy just to keep up with him. If the liturgy were totally, or even significantly, culturally dependent, then we could say that it would need continual revision. For with a changing material, plainly the form would have to be different too. But liturgy is not an expression of how people see things; rather it proposes, instead, how God sees all people.[12]

The reasons for submitting to liturgy are multitudinous and include conversion, thanksgiving, sacrifice, and praise. The results of liturgy are multitudinous and include forgiveness, mercy, strengthening, and communion. But at least one additional result is a reception of new sight. The liturgist comes away with the eye of the Dove, with a light that illuminates the world with divine perspective. Liturgy is not an expression of how people see things, liturgy in fact proposes how God sees all people, and to arrive at the point of seeing as God sees is the acquisition of a mystical vision. I do not mean the person has a vision of some mystical thing, I mean that the way the person sees is the way God sees, and that makes the liturgist's sight mystical. It is not a matter of seeing mystical things, it is a matter of seeing all things mystically. Where is God's sight revealed? In Scripture. Where is God's sight imparted, communicated, transmitted, bestowed? In liturgy. That's why liturgy is primary theology: here we absorb Scripture as Scripture. Living willingly under Christ's authority, we turn ourselves over to him to be formed and conditioned by him, and this is

---

[11] Paul Holmer, "About Liturgy and Its Logic," *Worship* 50, no. 1 (January 1976): 19.
[12] Holmer, "About Liturgy and Its Logic," 23.

why Holmer says liturgy has an element of formality.

Surely by "formal" Holmer does not mean "stuffy, prim, stiff," as my word processing thesaurus offers up. He is not arguing about a certain kind of style, but more arguing about those things he used to call in class a morphology, things that "create a form of life," what Wittgenstein called a "grammar." Forms permit meaning. There is the thing you want to say, and grammar allows you to say it—the grammatical form allows you to communicate your meaning. In this sense, formality abounds in social relationships because boundaries are set around the communal action so that things can be done; games are formal because there are rules that make the game possible; families are formal because the activities of eating supper together and reading bedtime books creates relational identities; the RCIA exists formally in order to develop a Christian character by bringing about a rule of life. Placing oneself under the formalities of families, cultures, games, logics, or lifestyles will create an identity. One does not first possess the identity and then go searching for a context in which to live it—rather, the reverse. Aidan Kavanagh would laconically say in class, "I don't go to Mass because I'm Catholic, I'm Catholic because I go to Mass." In writing he expressed it more completely: "Belief is always consequent upon the encounter with the Source of the grace of faith. Therefore Christians do not worship because they believe. They believe because the One in whose gift faith lies is regularly met in the act of communal worship—not because the assembly conjures up God, but because the initiative lies with the God who has promised to be there always. The *lex credendi* is thus subordinated to the *lex supplicandi*."[13]

So liturgy is formal. But what is the basis for this claim? Is Holmer simply making a generic claim about ritual behavior insofar as all sorts of groups create all sorts of identities through all sorts of rituals? No. He is not making a general claim about ritual, he is making a specific claim about liturgy, because the case of liturgy is unique. It is unique for the reason that it concerns our relationship with God. Because God is involved, liturgy is a unique case. Because this formality concerns God, therefore the liturgical grammar is not our invention, and the grammar by which we do liturgy must conform to God's logic or grammar. The apostle Paul therefore describes the grammar of Christian worship as *logike latreia* (Rom 12:1), which requires being

---

[13] Aidan Kavanagh, *On Liturgical Theology* (New York: Pueblo, 1984), 91.

formally harmonized to the Logos of God. Paul was playing on a distinction the Greeks made between *dulia* and *latria* that Holmer further explains. "Dulia" means homage paid to distinguished personages or places (the Archangel Gabriel gets dulia, Augustine gets dulia, maybe the grotto at the University of Notre Dame gets dulia), but "latria" is what we give God, and only God, because he is God. Holmer writes, "It is as if God being what he is, therefore all of us must be worshipful."[14] One can give dulia to the emperor, but one *must* give latria to God. Worshipfulness is the form of liturgy. Devotion, reverence, piousness, veneration, faithfulness is the form of liturgy because these are expressions that only God deserves, and he determines the form under which he receives them. If someone confused categories and gave latria to an emperor, it would be idolatry (i.e., giving latria to an *eidolon*, to an image instead of to the true God). Curiously enough, our idolatry can either create a god who is too soft on us or a god who is too hard on us. Some false images of God we carry in our minds need to be hardened by justice, others softened by mercy. I don't know which mistake we commit more often. Sometimes we create an idol who approves us at every turn, never contradicting our plans, never conflicting with our will, always supporting any decision we have already made—what good is a religion like that? What satisfaction would such a liturgy give? And sometimes we create an idol who is only fearsome, who never relents, whose face is as distant as it is impassive while it punishes and disapproves—what good is a religion like that? What happiness would such a liturgy give?

But the primary point Holmer is pushing is that whether we give latria or dulia to God does not depend upon how we feel. It's not up to us, it's in the nature of things. Early Christians realized that their worship "did not depend upon how the subject felt about the emperor or God. For dulia does not differ from latria by degree but in kind. The difference is determined by the objectivities involved, by one being a creature, though a mighty emperor, and the other being God. The object, not the subject, calls forth the proper kind of worship."[15] The mystery of liturgy, as it seizes hold of us, arises from the latria called forth by the object being worshipped (God) and does not arise from the subject worshipping (us). To say that liturgy is formal is to say that it is God who decides the form of liturgies; the character of

---

14 Holmer, "About Liturgy and Its Logic," 24.
15 Holmer, "About Liturgy and Its Logic," 19.

God obliges latria and not dulia; God defines the type of worship we should give; our worship should suit the character of God, we should not suit ourselves. The basis for the formality of liturgy is the transcendence of God. Once again, we are not here talking about a stylistic preference, rather we are saying that our worship must be latria because it is worship of the Creator, not a creature, and its formality comes from being an exercise in latria. This worship orders a certain kind of speech and a certain kind of activity.

Holmer thinks a sort of restlessness would ensue if liturgy were only dulia, and not latria, because then worship would be an expression of the subject (ourselves), and the subject is constantly changing. Sometimes we change for the better and feel closer to God, sometimes for the worse and feel more distant from God, but in either case, the worship would change as the state of the subject changes. If that were the case, then we could not judge any worship right or wrong, orthodox or heterodox, and we could not argue about its form and content, because the only criterion by which to judge self-expression is the sincerity of the person's expression. And it is just such an idea that Holmer sets out to contradict. "An odd thing about liturgy, then, is that it has to conform to this God. If it does not, it can easily become both a folly and an abomination in God's sight."[16] We have only to look to the Old Testament prophets to confirm this. They are not shy about condemning the worship that occurs in the temple if that temple worship does not conform to Yahweh. Therefore Holmer concludes that

> [t]he notion that a liturgy might be an expression of how people feel is surely not a defensible consideration. . . . The only criterion is not whether it works or whether it turns people on. In fact if it did, it might be a little dubious. For getting "turned on" is an expression that belongs to Old Glory, to sex, to heroics, to childhood memories, and even to the exceedingly boisterous Hallelujah Chorus as we so often encounter it. . . .

> But it would be odd to say that Christian worship and liturgy are only stimulating or expressive. For worship requires not that one like the liturgy but that one come to abide in God

---

[16] Holmer, "About Liturgy and Its Logic," 22.

himself. To worship God requires that one really worship him and not get engrossed in the liturgy. The liturgy gets its legitimacy and point from the fact that God requires an offering, enjoins contrition and repentance, promises a pardon, and proffers redemption. But this makes sense only because there is a God whose will is our law, whose pardon is our renewed life, and whose mercy reads our very hearts.[17]

Insofar as our latria must be fitted to God, it is God who must determine the contours of our worship. Then it will be mystical worship!

There is a God whose will is our law. There is a God whose will is also the law of our prayer—he establishes the *lex* of our *orandi*. The Catechism says, "If from the beginning Christians have celebrated the Eucharist and *in a form whose substance has not changed* despite the great diversity of times and liturgies, it is because we know ourselves to be bound by the command the Lord gave on the eve of his Passion: 'Do this in remembrance of me' [*1 Cor* 11:24–25]."[18] Liturgy is where we learn to know God mystically. It is like the grammar within which sentences take form, the logic within which meaning takes form, the rules within which lives take form. It is an abiding *lex orandi* whose purpose is to make us into liturgical people. What Holmer calls the "formality of liturgy" reveals the one alone to whom we must go.

It is only for a God like that, whose grace is our boundary and whose pleasure is a life of glory for us that a liturgy makes sense. No wonder, thusly, that only that God, not just any god, can mend our broken lives, pardon our sins, and, finally, redeem our careers. We cannot beg forgiveness for our sins from anyone else; we cannot pray for mercy to just anyone who happens by. The thorough and total humbling that true worship becomes is also our surest way to know the true God.[19]

Liturgical latria trains us in a posture or attitude or disposition or capacity which is required in order to know the mysteries of God.

---

[17] Holmer, "About Liturgy and Its Logic," 21.

[18] *Catechism of the Catholic Church*, 1356. Emphasis added. Hereafter cited in text as "*CCC*."

[19] Holmer, "About Liturgy and Its Logic," 22.

A popular expectation of "the mysterious" is to spellbind, allure, captivate a person. We expect a mystery to engross and beguile and charm, and this is not far from the truth, but it is only a portion of the truth—the part that lies at the conclusion on the far end. At the outset, to be mystical the liturgy must be *enthralling*, and this is less comfortable than we think. To *enthrall* means to make a person a *thrall*: to put someone into bondage, to reduce someone to the condition of a captive, to enslave, to subjugate and make subservient. The apostle Paul describes himself as a *doulos*, someone who belongs to another (Rom 1:1; Titus 1:1), and the highest dignity he can imagine is to be a believer who willingly lives under Christ's authority (1 Cor 7:22; Col 4:12; Gal 1:10). When we come before God in liturgy, we come to serve him, we are bound to him, en-thralled, we become his mystical *doulos*. If we do not, then it is not God we are worshipping. In liturgy, we are God's slave, he is not ours. C. S. Lewis tells us that when the mare Hwin met Aslan for the first time in the *Chronicles of Narnia* she trotted up to the lion, shaking all over with fear, and said, "Please, you're so beautiful. You may eat me if you like. I'd sooner be eaten by you than fed by anyone else."[20] Has not Hwin just summarized every description that every mystic gives of every encounter with the Almighty? And has she not also described the pathway of asceticism? Liturgical asceticism that derives from latria is the preference to be eaten by God over being fed by any of the tantalizing goods the world has to offer. Hwin has made clear whence the posture of liturgical mysticism comes. Had she approached in some other way, with some other attitude, on some other terms, it would have been because she mistook Aslan for an ordinary lion, when, in fact, it should be Aslan, not Hwin, who determines her behavior. Liturgy that is latria, and not mere dulia, will enthrall us, enslave us, make us bond-servants, subjugate us to God. All the mystics have experienced this. They do not approach God with utilitarian and selfish concerns, they approach God because they are enthralled and ravished (i.e., seized and carried away by a mysterious force). We must not approach God in liturgy with practical and egocentric performances, we must approach him in worship because his divinity demands our mystical latria. Our liturgy must conform to God the way an icon conforms to its prototype, the way a *sacramentum* conforms to its *res*, the way a mask conforms to the

---

[20] C. S. Lewis, *The Horse and His Boy*, in *The Chronicles of Narnia*, complete set (New York: HarperCollins, 2001), 299.

face. God's countenance shows itself in the liturgy, and our *lex orandi* conforms to his face. It is madness to think we can tame the Lion of Judah with our ritual catnip. Therefore, liturgical mysticism.

Liturgy is primary theology (*theologia prima*); for this, we must be capacitated by a discipline that prepares our souls for liturgy (liturgical asceticism); and the outcome of this askesis is union with God (liturgical mysticism). Liturgy is participation in the life of the Trinity; asceticism is the capacitation for this liturgical state; theology is union with God. We are brought by the mysteries into truth, beauty, and goodness (orthodoxy, liturgy, and holiness). This theological union is initiated by God, proffered in the sacraments, exercised communally by an ecclesial liturgical people, and experienced mystically by individual believers. That last is one possible definition of faith. Faith is not mere assent to a doctrine, it is a living relationship to certain events, events that can only be understood (theology) by participating in those mysteries (liturgy).

Schmemann complains that we have separated what should be a unity into parts and defines liturgical theology as its recovery.

> We need liturgical theology, viewed not as a theology of worship and not as a reduction of theology to liturgy, but as a slow and patient bringing together of that which was for too long a time and because of many factors broken and isolated—liturgy, theology, and piety, their reintegration within one fundamental vision.[21]

If separated, liturgy becomes ceremony, theology becomes an intellectual exercise, and piety loses its term of reference. If separated from liturgy, mysticism loses its term of reference.

> The goal of liturgical theology, as its very name indicates, is to overcome the fateful divorce between theology, liturgy and piety—a divorce which, as we have already tried to show elsewhere, has had disastrous consequences for theology as well as for liturgy and piety. It deprived liturgy of its proper understanding by the people, who began to see in it beautiful

---

[21] Alexander Schmemann, "Liturgical Theology, Theology of Liturgy, and Liturgical Reform," in *Liturgy and Tradition*, ed. Thomas Fisch (Crestwood, NY: St. Vladimir's Seminary Press, 1990), 46.

and mysterious ceremonies in which, while attending them, they take no real part. It deprived theology of its living source and made it into an intellectual exercise for intellectuals. It deprived piety of its living content and term of reference.[22]

Theology, liturgy, asceticism, and mysticism coincide in a perichoretic relationship where each makes room for the other and each makes the other possible. Piety is our dutiful conduct toward God, and this, as Holmer has been saying, must be revealed to us and not determined by us: piety must be *theological*. Gregory the Great said,

> Through the fear of the Lord, we rise to piety, from piety then to knowledge, from knowledge we derive strength, from strength counsel, with counsel we move towards understanding, and with intelligence towards wisdom and thus, by the sevenfold grace of the Spirit, there opens to us at the end of the ascent the entrance to the life of Heaven.[23]

Fear of the Lord is a profound reverence for Almighty God, such as Holmer was describing, and it motivates us to avoid sin and attachment to all created things. Liturgy is the basis of asceticism. The definition of fear of the Lord is "to give filial worship to God precisely as our Father and to relate with all people as children of the same Father."[24] The gift of piety fosters spiritual dispositions like filial respect for God and a generous love for others arising from loving obedience toward the commandments of God. The faithfulness of the incarnate Son toward his Father is the model, and it is shared with us in his mysteries-made-present: *piety must be liturgical*. It is not easy for us to put away our self-love and commit perfect latria: *piety must be ascetical*. And whatever progress we make will come not of our own strength but from the Holy Spirit: *piety must be mystical*.

Kavanagh distinguishes primary theology from secondary theology and concludes "the true primary theologian in the Church is

---

[22] Alexander Schmemann, *Of Water and the Spirit* (Crestwood, NY: St. Vladimir's Seminary Press, 1974), 12.

[23] Gregory the Great, *Homilies on Ezekiel* II.7.7, quoted in John Paul II, *Letter to Priests* (Holy Thursday 1998), no. 3, http://w2.vatican.va/content/john-paul-ii/en/letters/1998/documents/hf_jp-ii_let_31031998_priests.html.

[24] Jordan Aumann, *Spiritual Theology* (New York: Bloomsbury Continuum, 2018), 97.

the liturgical assembly."[25] Liturgical theology is written with incense and icon and temple and feast and sacrament and relic. The liturgical life of the Church is her theology, because in the liturgy we have an experience that transforms us—not unlike the transforming experience Jacob had at the foot of the heavenly ladder, or Moses had at the burning bush, or Hwin had when Aslan revealed himself at last. Kavanagh analyzes what happens, as if by a slow-motion camera:

> [W]hat results in the first instance from such an experience is deep change in the very lives of those who participate in the liturgical act. And deep change will affect their next liturgical act, however slightly. To detect that change in the subsequent liturgical act will be to discover where theology has passed, rather as physics detects atomic particles in tracks of their passage through a liquid medium. . . . The results of this adjustment shows in the gradual evolution of the liturgical rites themselves. . . . It is the adjustment which is theological in all this. I hold that it is theology being born, theology in the first instance. It is what tradition has called *theologia prima*.[26]

In other words, there is a theological grammar to be learned from the Church's liturgy, and that formal grammar creates a mystic (though we must still trace some ascetical steps in between). To learn the language of primary theology, one must be saturated with the Church's *lex orandi* (i.e., with the Christian mystical form of life, which is faith). Then the Church's primary theology will be embodied in a mystic and condition how he thinks, how he feels, how he sees the world, how he speaks. Liturgy teaches us the grammar by which we can speak about God; even more, it teaches us the grammar by which we speak to God. Evagrius of Pontus calls prayer theology: "If you are a theologian you truly pray. If you truly pray you are a theologian."[27] (And before there were universities with theology faculties, there were theologians.) Learning to speak a language requires immersion into the form of life that enables the speech, the mystical

---

25 Kavanagh, *On Liturgical Theology*, 150.
26 Kavanagh, *On Liturgical Theology*, 73–74.
27 Evagrius, *The Pratikos & Chapters on Prayer* (Kalamazoo: Cistercian Publications, 1981), 60.

life. The liturgy is celebrated by mystics. The Church forms mystical theologians by their formal liturgical life in latria. Mysticism is the oxygen that liturgy–theology–piety breathes.

If liturgy were our dulia expression, and not God's latria command, then it would be absolutely absurd to say that "the law of prayer establishes the law of belief" (*lex orandi supplicandi lex credendi*). The maxim only makes sense if liturgy is revelatory (i.e., a mystical movement of God among us). Kavanagh says, "Liturgy and Word are the foundational form the grace of God takes when it works itself out within our social midst. Liturgy no less than Word is of God. Only on this basis can the *lex supplicandi* be said to found and constitute the *lex credendi*."[28] "To reverse the maxim, subordinating the standard of worship to the standard of belief, makes a shambles of the dialectic of revelation."[29] Schmemann says, "[I]t is not the Church that exists for, or 'generates,' the liturgy, it is the Eucharist which, in a very real sense, 'generates' the Church, makes her to be what she is."[30] The liturgy gives the Church her identity, because "the Church itself is a *leitourgia*, a ministry, a calling to act in this world after the fashion of Christ, to bear testimony to him and His kingdom."[31] Notice his phrasing. Not that the Church *has* a liturgy, or *does* a liturgy, but that the Church *is* a liturgy, which means that her very existence is a manifestation of the new age as she acts after the fashion of Christ. This is mystical conformity to Christ. The Church *is* liturgical mysticism. Church-at-liturgy is a playground for mystics. When the early Christians chose the word *leitourgia* to describe what they do on the Lord's day, the eighth day, they signaled that they were not thinking of a dulia that was their particular religious cult; instead they were thinking of the latria that should be offered to the Creator, as all the stars and animals do, as heaven and earth does, and as Jesus, the only begotten Son of God does, and has taught us to do, and empowers us to do, as he joins us to himself to do. The latreutic liturgy of the Church is not just another one of Adam's cults, it is the cult of the New Adam (Christ's relationship with the Father) mystically perpetuated in us. The liturgist's liturgy is not classified as one species in

---

[28] Kavanagh, *On Liturgical Theology*, 123.
[29] Kavanagh, *On Liturgical Theology*, 92.
[30] Alexander Schmemann, "Theology and Eucharist," in *Liturgy and Tradition*, ed. Thomas Fisch (Crestwood, NY: St. Vladimir's Seminary Press, 1990), 79.
[31] Schmemann, "Theology and Eucharist," 79.

the genus of religious ritual. The liturgist's liturgy is mystical. The liturgist's liturgy is the activity of the mystical body of Christ, or the activity of Christ in his mystical body.

The priesthood exercised in the liturgy is not our own, it is Christ's priesthood shared with us in two modes, common and ministerial. Pius XII noted that the liturgy is "nothing more nor less than the exercise of [Christ's] priestly function."[32] And the Constitution on the Sacred Liturgy from the Second Vatican Council says, "Rightly, then, the liturgy is considered as an exercise of the priestly office of Jesus Christ."[33] And the Catechism of the Catholic Church expresses the same thought:

> The word "liturgy" originally meant a "public work" or a "service in the name of/on behalf of the people." In Christian tradition it means the participation of the People of God in "the work of God" [Cf. *Jn* 17:4]. Through the liturgy Christ, our redeemer and high priest, continues the work of our redemption in, with, and through his Church. (*CCC* 1069)

If we run *leitourgia* all the way upstream to its headwaters, we will find it coming from the Trinity, well said in Pius XII's definition: "The sacred liturgy is, consequently, the public worship which our Redeemer as Head of the Church renders to the Father, as well as the worship which the community of the faithful renders to its Founder, and through Him to the heavenly Father. It is, in short, the worship rendered by the Mystical Body of Christ in the entirety of its Head and members."[34] Liturgy is the work of a few on behalf of the many, and in this case, to be precise, it is the work of three—Father, Son, and Holy Spirit—on behalf of the human race, which requires redemption. That is the work that Christ came to do for the human race, that is, the work (*leitourgia*) into which someone is baptized when he or she is made co-participant in his liturgy. The Father's will is to destroy death and raise us to eternal life, and this he accomplishes through the Son and Holy Spirit. It happens already, at this hour, for sin is a

---

[32] Pius XII, Encyclical on the Sacred Liturgy *Mediator Dei* (November 20, 1947), §22.

[33] Paul VI, Constitution on the Sacred Liturgy *Sacrosanctum Concilium* (December 4, 1963), §7.

[34] Pius XII, *Mediator Dei*, §20.

state of death (i.e., being cut off from God, the source of life) and to be restored to that source is the mystical work of God. Liturgical life means immersion in the mystical age of the Spirit (it is spiritual life). Mystical life means the Holy Spirit makes us liturgical apprentices to Jesus as the High Priest. The Church's belief, her *lex credendi*, is revealed in her life, and the rules that govern that life are contained in the Church's liturgical *ordo*, her *lex orandi*. Liturgy, theology, and piety intertwine in every baptized believer's mystical identity.

Holmer critiques a state of mind he calls "liturgical hyperconsciousness," which I would simply characterize as looking *at* the liturgy instead of looking *through* the liturgy. A person can look at a window, or through a window, but the whole point of "formality" is that we shouldn't be looking at it, it should be allowing us to look at realities. We should be unaware of the grammar that organizes the sentence and get on with expressing the meaning we intend, we should be unaware of the rules that organize the game and get on with playing it. Holmer applies this to liturgy by saying, "The liturgy is like the logic of life within which each of us must learn to improvise."[35] He warns against liturgical hyperconsciousness because "no believer ought to be conscious of the liturgy when the aim of the liturgy is to make one conscious of God. . . . After all, it is a little absurd to be reverent toward the practices and then forget about being reverent to God."[36] It is a little absurd to be reverent toward the liturgy but fail to be a mystic. A dose of liturgical mysticism might forestall the liturgical narcissism one sometimes encounters. Latreutic liturgy is adoration that devoutly recognizes God's transcendent excellence and results in self-abasement before the Infinite. It is a mystical move made not just by those favored with extraordinary graces but by all who grow into liturgical persons participating through the Spirit in the Son's adoration of the Father.

It is the nature of love to give itself to an other, to ecstatically (kenotically) turn out toward the other, as parents do toward their children, as a lover does toward his beloved, as the Triune God did toward us. Thus begins the story of the divine economy, which can be told in three chapters. First, God extended himself in love by creating non-divine beings, and then into that creation God came. Natural law, theophanies, and epiphanies all witness to the fact that the *Logos*

---

[35] Holmer, "About Liturgy and Its Logic," 25.
[36] Holmer, "About Liturgy and Its Logic," 24.

was at work in the *logoi* strewn across creation. Second, as a result of pride and disobedience, the human reaction was anything but latria. The man and the woman hid themselves from the presence of the Lord God instead of offering up true worship. They fled the temple. Third, the Lord put on flesh—a final *kenosis*—and came down from the realm of the faithful angels to seek out the one lost sheep, the human race.

> The shepherd leaving the fold in the depths of night to plunge into the dark and lonely ravines of a mountain lying under a curse in search of the one lost sheep, is the Word stooping down, even to us. As if the immensity of the angelic world which had remained faithful was nothing to him and the Father in comparison . . . we see him coming forth from his Father's house and going down to the deepest part of the chasm. Sharing all the sufferings, stripping himself of his divine glory, he finds the sheep in the abyss. Then he lifts it on his shoulders and, bent under the burden, retracing the painful road which it had trodden, it brings it back to the fold. As they both come in sight of the sheepfold, shepherd and sheep covered with the same wounds, their blood mingling, the unanimous joy of the faithful sheep, who are always present in the Father's site, is transfigured.[37]

Mysticism is surfing the wave crest of Christ's ascension, and it is liturgical because *kenosis* and ascension make up the two moving parts of the liturgy being celebrated.

Liturgical mysticism is being grasped by Christ's fastened grip, as the icons of the Anastasis show the risen Jesus grasping Adam and Eve's wrist to pull them out of the grave. Being restored to the cycle of agape and *eucharistia* is liturgical mysticism wherein we find our mystical breath again. And it does not begin post-mortem, it begins post-baptism (a spiritual death). This is the fundamental mystery celebrated in the liturgy, though one frequently overlooked. Grace creates the capacity for a person to respond and cooperate with grace, as Augustine observed. "God made you without any cooperation on your part. You did not lend your consent so that God could make you. How

---

[37] Louis Bouyer, *The Meaning of the Monastic Life* (London: Burns & Oates, 1955), 34–35.

could you have consented, when you did not exist? But he who made you without your consent does not justify you without your consent. He made you without your knowledge, but he does not justify you without your willing it."[38] Augustine is making a nod toward asceticism. Liturgical asceticism is the work of conversion that baptism releases into our lives, the training for death and resurrection that we undergo daily, our transformation from a carnal person into a mystical person. Holmer says, "The liturgy does not have to carry people all the way; and trying to contrive it so that it will, violates both the gospel and our fragile spiritual balance. God has refused to let things external and public carry us all the way to the goals he has set before us. Our will, affections, and habits must also be changed, and God himself still leaves a great deal for each of us to do on his own."[39]

Liturgy is heaven on earth, liturgists are mystics, and these liturgical mystics undergo the asceticism which is the cost of being made Christoform in order to commit liturgy. The parts of the Christian life—liturgy, theology, asceticism—interweave mystically with each other like dancers round the Maypole. Liturgy is participation by the body of Christ through the Holy Spirit in the Son's bond with the Father; asceticism is the capacitation for that participation, called deification; the whole aim of asceticism is to capacitate a person for prayer; the highest experience of prayer is theologia; "theologia" is union with God as it exists at the conclusion of asceticism; the deified life is a mystical state; primary theology is a kind of knowing that requires a deep change in the mind (*nous*) of the knower—a *meta-nous* (metanoia, repentance, for the Kingdom of God is at hand); such *metanoia* is ascetical and it capacitates for liturgy. Liturgical mysticism is the *praxis* of eschatological life. Then liturgy can be mystical act.

Holmer converted the noun "capacity" into the verb "capacitate" when he studied how subjects (persons) were created. In his world of discourse, capacity did not mean a vacant space, like some empty stage behind the curtain. Rather, it meant the process of fulfilling a potential—more like staging the set on which you will act out your life. Being capacitated is growing into a more complete person, cultivating a form of life, weaving things into the texture of one's life. A capacity is different from a skill or activity by the fact that it must be done by

---

[38] Augustine, *Sermons* 169.13, in W. A. Jurgens, *The Faith of the Fathers*, vol. 3 (Collegeville: Liturgical Press, 1970), 29.

[39] Holmer, "About Liturgy and Its Logic," 25.

the lifetime, and not only by the hour. I can read from two 'til three, but it would be odd to say I will understand from two 'til three, because reading is a skill or activity, and understanding is a capacity. Capacities operate steadily and persistently below the surface, undergirding the person in all that he or she does, and being capacitated means receiving formation at that level. Our Christian identity comes from the acquisition of capacities that become deep-seated and controlling dispositions in us. In another place Holmer writes, "What we know depends upon the kind of person we have made ourselves to be."[40] Conversion consists of becoming a new person, learning new passions and training our wants, being re-capacitated, being re-capitulated as we are en-thralled to a new head. There are things that can only be known by becoming a new kind of person. Therefore, if Christ is ever going to teach us that the Father is love, he will do so not by stating the fact over and over but by making us into loving people; therefore, if Christ is ever going to teach us the mysteries he came to reveal, he will do so not by explaining them over and over but by taking us up into those mysteries; therefore, if Christ is going to teach us the spiritual life, he will walk us through the desert of liturgical asceticism to the promised land where we can live as liturgical people. Liturgical asceticism is the struggle to imitate what we see in every liturgy, and in every liturgy we see a human being named Jesus living in filial communion with God the Father.

Every liturgical assembly is as filled with the Holy Spirit as was that first assembly at Pentecost. The interior spirit must find peace from the passions (liturgical asceticism) in order to stand before the burning bush and catch fire (liturgical mysticism), which is possible in every liturgical experience of the Church (liturgical theology). That is why we are thrown into liturgy week after week, year after year, like a stone is thrown into a rock tumbler for polishing. Liturgy has an abiding and formal *lex orandi* that capacitates liturgical persons. We do not change the ancient themes of liturgy, they change us— into mystical persons. The liturgy's formality exists so that we can learn the actions of latria in the public sacramental liturgy, and we go Sunday after Sunday to apprehend our personal liturgy, and stand aright before God, and keep the liturgical year and its feasts, and exercise the sacramentals in every nook of our lives, and let the prayer of the Church pass through our lips in Divine Office—all so we can

---

[40] Paul Holmer, *C. S. Lewis: His Life and His Thought* (New York: Harper & Row, 1976), 90.

hear God pronouncing our mystical name over and over again, a little more clearly each time.

CHAPTER 2

ORDINARY LITURGICAL MYSTICISM

I AM IDENTIFYING two underpinnings to liturgical mysticism. The first, treated last chapter, is the idea that liturgists should be mystics, enthralled by—made captive to—Christ, the high heavenly priest, the one whose liturgical life we absorb. Liturgical mysticism discerns liturgy as something more deep and serious than our own human construction. Liturgical mysticism affects ecclesiology because our experience of the mysteries of Christ in liturgy makes clear to us that the Church is his Body in Mystery, always hearing his mystical word and feeding upon his mystical body. The second, to be treated this chapter, is the idea that mysticism is ordinary for Christians. To make the point, I must begin by going back to liturgical asceticism. Although the monk leaves the world to become a desert ascetic, he is an extraordinary witness to the discipline the baptized Christian should practice in the world as a secular ascetic. Likewise, although the exceptional mystic may leave the world in states of ecstasy, he is an extraordinary witness to the spirituality the baptized Christian should practice in the world as a mundane mystic.

Olivier Clément defines *askesis* as "an awakening from the sleep-walking of daily life. It enables the Word to clear the silt away in the depth of the soul, freeing the spring of living waters. . . . It is the Word who acts, but we have to co-operate with him, not so much by the exertion of will-power as by loving attentiveness."[1] Spirituality

---

[1]   Olivier Clément, *The Roots of Christian Mysticism* (Hyde Park, NY: New City

23

can be generically defined as some sort of interior conversation. One becomes conscious of oneself (which is different from being self-conscious) because one makes time for considering internal things and is not totally preoccupied with external things. Asceticism is watchfulness, wakefulness, loving vigilance over our interior conversation by which we become philosophically observant of vices and virtues. But eventually we may become aware of God's resolute desire to be let into that interior conversation. Instead of knocking down the door to our interior heart, God knocks at the door to the interior heart, kenotically sheathing his power and requesting permission to enter. The visitation and fiat that Mary experienced happens over and over again. Grace is the engine of asceticism and leads us to take our first baby steps in liturgy, and grace is gentle, though relentless. Its aim, says Evdokimov, "is the reconstruction in us of the image of God (*imago Dei*), of our initial form, tending toward God, as a copy of the Original."[2] When the liturgical circulation of agape and glory resumes in our hearts, then we are guided into the unitive state called "theologia," but hearts that are distorted by pride must be converted in order to do liturgy.

It is just barely possible that not everyone thinks, as I do, that asceticism is mystical in nature. It is just barely possible that some people think, as I do not, that asceticism is a chore, negative in nature, while mysticism is a reward, positive in nature. Reginald Garrigou-Lagrange dedicated several volumes to repudiating this position, which he thinks was a mistake that entered Western theology in the seventeenth and eighteenth centuries. Under this error, ordinary Christians are thought to be only concerned with ascetical theology, while only extraordinary Christians are thought to be concerned with mystical theology and extraordinary graces. In other words, asceticism stops short of mysticism and reposes at a lower level.

> From this point of view, asceticism does not lead to mysticism, and the perfection, or 'ordinary' union, to which it leads, is normally an end [in itself] and not a disposition to a more intimate and more elevated union. Hence mystical theology is of importance only to some very rare, privileged

---

Press, 1996), 130, 131.

[2] Paul Evdokimov, *Ages of the Spiritual Life* (Crestwood, NY: St. Vladimir's Press, 1998), 192.

souls; we may just as well, then, almost ignore it in order to avoid presumption and confusion.[3]

Garrigou-Lagrange thinks those who separated ascetical theology from mystical theology did so out of a combined eagerness to system-ize things and to remedy abuses. "According to their point of view, ascetical theology treats of the exercises which lead to perfection ac-cording to the ordinary way, whereas mystical theology treats of the extraordinary way, to which the infused contemplation of the myster-ies of faith would belong."[4]

If this were the case, then the ordinary liturgical theologian whom Kavanagh called Mrs. Murphy would be precluded from three identities: she could not be a theologian for not being an academic, she could not be an ascetic for not being a vowed religious, and she could not be a mystic for not having extraordinary graces. I wish to challenge this and instead present Mrs. Murphy as a liturgical mys-tic.[5] Being a liturgically formed ascetic, she has learned the *theologia prima* from the *lex orandi* of liturgy and is an ordinary, normal, Chris-tian liturgical mystic. Kavanagh calls such an ascetical-sanctified life stunningly normal.

> This is a life expected of every one of the baptized, whose ultimate end is the same supreme beatitude. It is a life all the baptized share, a life within which the professed ascetic is nothing more or less than a virtuoso who serves the whole community as an exemplar of its own life. The ascetic is simply a stunningly normal person who stands in constant witness to the normality of Christian *orthodoxia* in a world flawed into abnormality by human choice.[6]

[3] Reginald Garrigou-Lagrange, *Christian Perfection and Contemplation* (St. Louis, MO: B. Herder, 1945), 28.

[4] Reginald Garrigou-Lagrange, *The Three Ages of the Interior Life*, vol. 1 (London: Catholic Way, 2014), 30.

[5] It seems understood by people that the baptized Christian exercises a royal priest-hood, though not of the ordained variety. It is a puzzle to me why people find it difficult to understand that Mrs. Murphy is theologian, ascetic, and mystic when it is taken for granted that she has a baptismal priesthood.

[6] Aidan Kavanagh, *On Liturgical Theology* (New York: Pueblo, 1984), 161–162.

The holiness and mystery offered to all the baptized as an objective gift will be lived out in an exceptional manner by some specially graced mystics, just as asceticism will be lived out in an exceptional manner by some gifted monks, but the ascetic in the desert does not do anything the baptized person is not also supposed to do, he only does it differently, and likewise the extraordinary mystic does not know a different reality than is known by the baptized person, he only knows it with a different force and a different charisma, granted him by God in order to serve the whole community as virtuosic exemplar. Asceticism leads to theologia, which is union with God in the mystical body living from its liturgy. So John Behr's study leads him to conclude that asceticism "was not a detachable dimension of Christian life, a specialized technique . . . or the domain of the monastics. Rather, asceticism was the realization, the putting into practice, of the new eschatological life granted in baptism within the confines of the present life."[7] Liturgical asceticism is the *terminus a quo* of a liturgical mystic.

Certainly we recognize extraordinary, graced mystics. We also recognize virtuosic, professed ascetics. And we recognize genius, scholastic theologians as well. They are *unusual*, in the sense of being out of the ordinary and rare. But it is *normal* for a baptized Christian to be a mystic, an ascetic, and a theologian, in the sense of natural, ordered, and something you should expect. Garrigou-Lagrange considers the infused contemplation of the mysteries of faith to be "the normal way of sanctity and to be morally necessary to the full perfection of Christian life."[8] Froget proposes,

> [T]he soul of every person, no matter when he lived or what degree of holiness he acquired, whether he attained to the very heights of perfection or whether he was but entering upon the road of righteousness, whether an adult or an infant is united with God through grace, and entertains the Holy Spirit as his Guest. True, this union can be more or less perfect, it can admit of degrees which vary *ad infinitum*, but the mystical union is everywhere and always essentially the same.[9]

---

[7] John Behr, *Asceticism and Anthropology in Irenaeus and Clement* (Oxford: Oxford University Press, 2000), 17.

[8] Garrigou-Lagrange, *The Three Ages of the Interior Life*, 1:2.

[9] Barthelemy Froget, *The Indwelling of the Holy Spirit in the Souls of the Just According to the Teaching of St. Thomas Aquinas* (New York: Paulist Press, 1921), 118.

Here is an illustration. White light contains all the colors of the spectrum, and a rainbow is only seen when that white light is refracted through a prism. Jesus Christ is the light of the world, eternally streaming forth from the Father as the only begotten Son and flashing his light upon us through the power of the Holy Spirit. By his hypostatic union, he unites heaven and earth, eternity and the temporal, the Creator and the created. That single brilliant light suffuses his whole Church, but upon passing through a historical prism, it can be dispersed into a spectrum of saints. The baptismal illumination contains theology, asceticism, and mysticism (as white light contains all the other colors) before it is broken by a specialized prism, for specialized needs, into extraordinary examples. *Lumen Gentium* affirms the universal call to holiness of all the faithful, of whatever rank or status, since the "Lord Jesus, the divine Teacher and Model of all perfection, preached holiness of life to each and every one of His disciples of every condition."[10] Christ's brilliance illuminates the ordinary Christian saint, even if afterward this light can be refracted into a rainbow of married and celibates, theologians and contemplatives, patrons and beggars, monks and martyrs and mystics. Karl Adam provides a longer list.

How exceedingly various are the ways by which they followed Christ, and how manifold their forms of saintliness. By the side of the saintly hermit and the ascetic of the desert stands the social saint, the saint of the great city and of the industrial classes. By the side of the foreign missionary stands the saint who gave his life to cripples, or idiots, or to the criminals condemned to the galleys. By the side of the saint who is arrayed in robe of penance and rough girdle, stands the saint of the salon, the refined and saintly man of the world. By the side of the saint of strict enclosure and constant silence stands the joyous friar, who calls the swallow his sister and the moon his brother. By the side of the saint of divine learning stands the saint who despised all knowledge save of Christ. By the side of the contemplative mystic, the world-conquering apostle. By the side of the saint who does penance in filth and rags, and values ignominy beyond all things else, stands the

---

[10] Paul VI, Dogmatic Constitution on the Church *Lumen Gentium* (November 21, 1964), §40.

saint robed in imperial purple and crowned with the glory of the tiara. By the side of the saint who fights and is slain for his faith, stands the saint who suffers and dies for it. By the side of the innocent saint stands the penitent. By the side of the saint of child-like meekness, the saint who must wrestle with God until He bless Him.

How infinitely various are all these saintly figures! Each one is marked with the stamp of his own time, some very plainly so. There are many, indeed, with whom we can no longer establish any genuinely sympathetic contact. For there is but One who is ever modem, never out of date, One only who belongs to all time.[11]

This explains why Catholics are not envious or jealous toward saints and mystics who possess extraordinary graces, why they are not embarrassed to be around them, why they are glad to see virtuosic performances of the Gospel. Rivalry is precluded by the communion of love between the saints and by the beatitude that comes from obedience to God. Every person should be full of the glory appropriate to his state of life, but states of life are different. Dorothy Sayers comments on this in Dante's description of heaven, but it is no less true already on earth.

> There is equality in the sense that all the souls alike are as full of bliss as they are capable of being: but between soul and soul there is no formal equality at all. The pint-pot and the quart-pot are *equally full*: but there is no pretence that a pint and a quart are the same thing; neither does the pint-pot ever dream of saying to the quart-pot, "I'm as good as you are"— still less of saying "It isn't fair that you should hold more than I." The old sin of Envy . . . is utterly extinguished in Heaven.[12]

Thus, when Dante asks one of the saints in the lower Heaven, "Do you long to go higher, to gain more knowledge or win for yourselves more love?" she laughs, and all the blessed laugh with her, and she replies in the famous lines, "Brother, our desires are stilled by love. We want only what we have. To want more would be discordant with the will

---

[11] Karl Adam, *The Spirit of Catholicism* (New York: Angelico Press, 2012), 240.

[12] Dorothy Sayers, *Introductory Papers on Dante* (Eugene, OR: Wipf & Stock, 2006), 57.

of Him who disposes us here, and in these circles there is no room for that, for here our being is in charity and cannot be otherwise."[13] The baptized Christian, with his or her royal mysticism, has a desire stilled by love and is not envious of the spectacular mystic—from *spectaculum,* meaning a sight or show, a visible witness that God judged necessary for the world at a particular time, for a particular purpose.

The mystical life is the normal crowning of Christian faith. Have you faith? Then Columba Marmion insists that you have a mysterious, mystical, supernatural knowledge. Faith is "the light that reveals the Divine thoughts to us and makes us penetrate into God's designs."[14] And this is more than ratiocination about doctrinal propositions. It is participatory knowledge. "What in fact is faith? It is a mysterious participation in the knowledge that God has of Himself. God knows Himself as Father, Son, and Holy Spirit,"[15] and faith participates in this divine self-knowledge.

> When we contemplate the Incarnate Word at Bethlehem, let us rise above the things of sense so as to gaze upon him with the eyes of faith alone. Faith makes us share here below in the knowledge that the Divine Persons have of One Another. There is no exaggeration in this. Sanctifying grace makes us indeed partakers of the divine nature. Now, the activity of the divine nature consists in the knowledge that the Divine Persons have the One of the Other, and the love that they have One for the Other. We participate therefore in this knowledge and in this love. . . . Grace enables us to behold deep down into these mysteries through the eyes of God: *Lux tuae claritatis infulsit* [Preface for Christmas].[16]

---

13 Sayers, *Introductory Papers on Dante,* 57, referring to *Paradiso* III.70–72: "Brother, our will is stilled by the power of charity, which makes us wish only for what we have, nor do we thirst for anything beyond."

14 Columba Marmion, *Christ: The Ideal of the Monk* (London & Edinburgh: Sands; and St. Louis: Herder, 1922), 291–292. Or, again, "The Eternal Father presents His Word to the world: 'This is My beloved Son. . . . Hear ye him.' If we receive Him by faith, that is to say if we believe that he is the Son of God, the Word makes us partakers of the best that he has: His Divine Sonship; He shares with us His condition of Son, he gives us the grace of adoption; He gives us the right of calling God our Father." Columba Marmion, *Christ in His Mysteries* (St. Louis: B. Herder, 1931), 52.

15 Marmion, *Christ in His Mysteries,* 237.

16 Marmion, *Christ in His Mysteries,* 132.

Liturgy is the perichoresis of the Trinity kenotically extending itself until we have the knowledge each person has of the other, and the love each person has for the other, but on our own created level. This is the mystical knowledge into which we are initiated by liturgy.

We can make the question "What happens in liturgy?" more precise by asking "What happens *to us* in liturgy?" The former is speculative theology, the latter practical theology, and these two kinds of theology should always work in tandem. Here is John Chrysostom's answer to the latter question:

> Awful in truth are the Mysteries of the Church, awful in truth is the Altar. A fountain went up out of Paradise sending forth material rivers. From this table springeth up a fountain which sendeth forth rivers spiritual. By the side of this fountain are planted not fruitless willows, but trees reaching even to heaven, bearing fruit ever timely and undecaying. . . . This fountain is a fountain of light, spouting forth rays of truth. By it stand the Powers on high looking upon the beauty of its streams, because they more clearly perceive the power of the Things set forth, and the flashings unapproachable.[17]

A liturgical mystic swims this liturgical river upstream. Liturgy is the activity of the Church; the Church is the mystical body of Christ; liturgical mysticism is the activity of the mystical body of Christ as well as the activity of each individual member.

Jean Corbon utilizes the imagery of the river as it is found in Revelation 22: "In this final vision the seer of Patmos glimpses the indescribable energy of the Blessed Trinity at the heart of the messianic Jerusalem, that is, this Church of the last times in which we are now living. If we let the river of life permeate us, we become trees of life, for the mystery which the river symbolizes takes hold of us."[18] This energy of love flowing from the throne of God and the Lamb was at work before the world was created, Corbon says, and from the beginning of time the river of the mystery has watered the human earth.[19]

---

[17] John Chrysostom, Homily 46 on John 6:41–53, in *Nicene and Post-Nicene Fathers*, vol. 14, First Series, *Chrysostom: Homilies on the Gospel of Saint John and the Epistle to the Hebrews,* ed. Philip Schaff (Peabody, Massachusetts: Hendrickson, 2004), 167.

[18] Jean Corbon, *The Wellspring of Worship* (Mahaw, NJ: Paulist Press, 1988), 15.

[19] Corbon, *The Wellspring of Worship,* 16, 20.

But now the river is given a name. Christmas is the coming of the river of life in our flesh,[20] and thus "[t]he liturgy has been born; the resurrection of Jesus is its first manifestation. . . . This unprecedented power which the river of life exercises in the humanity of the risen Christ—that is the liturgy!"[21] While we wait to join the consummate liturgy in the heavenly Kingdom, the life-giving spring has already reached us: first it flows from heaven into the Church, and by the Church's mediation it overflows into the soul. This is the mediatorial quality of the Church. Christ has shared his liturgy with the Church and brought her to life; the Church mediates that liturgy to her individual members, bringing them to birth; when liturgy hypostasizes at the level of person, it is liturgical mysticism. Church liturgy is corporate, ritualized, symbolic; liturgical mysticism is personal, spiritualized, ascetical. The former requires institutions, the latter produces saints. The former sacramentally brings heaven to earth and offers Eucharistic food for consumption, characters for empowered mission, and healing for soul and body; the latter mystically translates a person from earth to heaven for his personal perfection. Liturgical mysticism is liturgy mystically energizing an individual member of the mystical body that the *leitourgia* has created. Jean Corbon calls the former "the liturgy celebrated" and the latter "the liturgy lived,"[22] but they are related insofar as the former makes the latter possible. By being baptized into the Church's sacramental liturgy we become liturgical persons whose lives are mystically illuminated by Christ, the light streaming forth from the Father.

When Jean Daniélou surveys every act of God, from alpha to omega, he does so by finding them to center around the home base of the Paschal mystery, toward which the whole game progresses.

> The Christian faith has only one object, the mystery of Christ dead and risen. But this unique mystery subsists under different modes: it is prefigured in the Old Testament, it is accomplished historically in the earthly life of Christ, it is contained in mystery in the sacraments, it is lived mystically in souls, it is accomplished socially in the Church, it is consummated eschatologically in the heavenly kingdom.[23]

---

20 Corbon, *The Wellspring of Worship*, 25.

21 Corbon, *The Wellspring of Worship*, 33–34.

22 Corbon, *The Wellspring of Worship*, section II and section III.

23 Jean Daniélou, "Le symbolism des rites baptismaux," *Dieu vivant*, quoted in Rob-

The river of life wells up from the mystery of Christ dead and risen; it brought its waters to the Church of the Old Testament, to the patriarchs and prophets, priests and kings; it flowed through Christ's life lived in glorification of his Father; and we continue to have access to this river through various sacramental means. The Christic river is found in both corporate sacramental liturgy and personal liturgical mysticism.

The liturgical activity of God is the Trinity's interior perichoresis of love inverting itself to make loving creatures who should respond to agape over the course of their ascent to deification. Or, in the summary words of the Catechism, "The grace of Christ is the gratuitous gift that God makes to us of his own life, infused by the Holy Spirit into our soul to heal it of sin and to sanctify it. It is the *sanctifying* or *deifying grace* received in Baptism" (CCC 1999). That paragraph is basically my definition of liturgy, with the added reminder that this power for deification is received in baptism. Mystical union with God is the consummation of humankind. It is what mankind was made for. It is where mankind should be going (had we not lost our head in the garden of Eden and required a re-capitulation—a reception of a new head, a New Adam). Daniélou therefore suggests we could sum up Christianity by connecting the doctrines of Trinity and deification and Christology:

> This is the heart and core of the irreducible originality of Christianity, that the Son of God came among us to reveal these two intimately related truths: that there is within God himself a mysterious living love, called the Trinity of Persons; and that in and through the Son we men are called to share this life of love. The mystery of the Holy Trinity, known to us through the Word made flesh, and the mystery of the deification of man in him—that is the whole of our religion, summed up in one person, the person of Jesus Christ.[24]

Christianity is the religion in which God became a human face in order to raise man up before the divine countenance. It is why Christ is the mediation of our contact with the Trinity, the basis of our liturgy, and the foundation of our mystical life.

---

ert Taft, "Toward a Theology of the Christian Feast," *Beyond East and West* (Rome: Pontifical Oriental Institute, 1997), 29.

[24] Jean Daniélou, *The Lord of History* (New York: Longmans, Green, 1958), 118.

The Council of Chalcedon established the ontological content of the Incarnation, but Benedict XVI notices that the Third Council of Constantinople still had to wrestle with the consequences of that content. The Pope emeritus says Constantinople had to ask, "What does 'one Person in two natures' mean for practical purposes? How can a person live with two wills and a dual intellect? And this is by no means just a matter of mere theoretical curiosity; this certainly also concerns ourselves in the form of the question: How can we live as baptized Christians?"[25] We know our Christology, but what does it have to do with us? What does Christ being fully human and fully divine mean for how we shall live? We know that we are saved by Christ, but what does it mean to be an actual member of his body? We know that Christ is the source of the river of liturgy, but besides asking what happens at liturgy, we want to ask what happens *to us* at liturgy. How can we live as baptized Christians? These are the questions of liturgical mysticism. They are questions of application, participation, pertinence, operation, connection, function, koinonia. The Council of Constantinople answered them by looking to Christ himself. Christian doctrine had already rejected the idea that there was no human will in Christ (Monothelitism); it had already rejected the idea that there were two separate spheres of willing (Nestorianism); Chalcedon had instead affirmed a communion (koinonia) of two wills. So Benedict XVI concludes, "On a practical level—existentially—the two wills become one single will, and yet ontologically they remain two independent entities."[26] This communion of wills that the Son has with the Father is the sort of mystical communion offered to someone baptized into Christ.

So when we talk about Christology and Trinity, we are not talking metaphysics (much less mathematics), we are talking soteriology. The sharing is so mystically complete that not only can we travel in the one direction, as we did at Constantinople when we journeyed from Christology to our identity as baptized Christians, but we can also travel in the reverse direction, starting with our experience of salvation and journeying to Christ's identity. Emile Mersch calls this the "soteriological argument," which can infer what the Savior must be from the work of salvation he accomplishes. We can infer something

---

[25] Joseph Ratzinger, *Pilgrim Fellowship of Faith: The Church As Communion* (San Francisco: Ignatius Press, 2005), 80–81.

[26] Ratzinger, *Pilgrim Fellowship*, 81.

about the cause from his effect. If Christ can bring this sort of person about, we know something about the sort of person he was. "So truly do we possess all things in common with Him, that from what we are it is possible to infer what He had to be, just as it is possible to see, from what He is, what we in turn are destined one day to be."[27] A mystical arc connects Bethlehem to every baptismal font, and we can travel either direction on it. Christology enters the realm of liturgical mysticism when the doctrine of Christ passes beyond historical fact into the existential plane of our lives and when the daily construction of our lives includes a mystical thread.

Our starting point for a mysticism that is liturgical, then, will not be rubric and ceremony. Our starting point for liturgical mysticism will be baptism. We discover liturgical mysticism lapping the shores of the baptismal font. Liturgical mysticism begins with entry into the perichoresis of the Trinity, an entry made possible by a synergistic descent and ascent that stamp Christ's incarnate life on us, a life we will recognize in the mystical dimensions of a converted existence begun by baptism. The Holy Spirit in-spires us; all apostolic ministry ex-pires him; and we have a synergistic con-spiracy of faith, hope, and charity with him that composes our mystical life. Why liturgical mysticism? Because liturgy is heaven's descension and mysticism is humanity's ascension.

I am speaking in spatial terms of ascent because our bodies occupy space and the speech is natural to us, but we know that heaven is not spatial. It is not temporal, either. Heaven is the milieu of mysticism. Heaven is newness, the recapitulation of man and woman, a new age of communion with God that the human race has not had from the time of its exile out of Eden until its revivification by the Paschal mystery. If we wish to continue in spatial terms, liturgical mysticism is the Eternal One sweeping us *up* to carry us *forward* and *inward*. "Up, forward, inward." Gregory the Great regularly uses these contrasts to help us grasp what heaven means. He contrasts *inward*

---

[27] Emile Mersch, *The Whole Christ: The Historical Development of the Doctrine of the Mystical Body in Scripture and Tradition* (Milwaukee: Bruce, 1938), 241. Here are two other formulations of the argument by Mersch: "That we may conclude from what the faithful are to what the Savior is, salvation must be a matter of mystical solidarity between ourselves and Him; we must be able to say in truth that men are saved only in virtue of their incorporation in the Savior" (317). "Indeed, the Incarnation has made Him so like us that we can judge what He is by simply reflecting upon what we ourselves are" (361).

with *outward, above* with *below,* and *then* with *now.* In our sinful state we tend to operate out of the second term in each of those pairings: we direct our life *outward* toward things that dazzle us at the *present* moment, even though they actually lie much *below* our dignity. We are distracted by superficial outer noises because in the Fall we have gone deaf to the celestial voices, and all we hear now is the Sirens of temporal materialism. Thus we mistakenly conclude that the world outside us is more important than the world within us; that this world below is the ultimate reality; and that the present passing moment is of more consequence than the spiritual compilation of eternal moments.

Gregory tries to break the illusion of this sinful life and instead offers us a vision of an *inward life* that rises *above* into what we will *know then.* Here is an example, in his words, of each breakthrough. First, a turn from outward to inward. "If we wish then to contemplate things within, let us rest from outward engagements. . . . For when the mind is at rest from outward employments, the weight of the Divine precepts is more fully discerned."[28] Second, a turn from below to above. "For the human creature by this alone, that it is a creature, has it inherent in itself to sink down below itself, but man has obtained it from his Creator, that he should both be caught above himself by contemplation, and held fast in himself by incorruption."[29] Third, a lifting of our eyes from now to then. "The Church of the Elect will then be fully day, when the shade of sin will be no longer blended with it. It will then be fully day, when it has been brightened with the perfect warmth of the inward light."[30] Mystical life is inward, above, and to come, in contrast to carnal life, which is outward, below, and now.

Yet, despite the contrast seen by Gregory in each pair, he is able to combine them in ways that confound simplistic thinking about heaven. Each metaphor—spatial, interior, and temporal—modifies the other and keeps us off-base. If we think of heaven *above,* he tells us it is within; if we think of heaven *within,* he tells us it is still to come; if we think heaven is *then,* he tells us the Kingdom is already present. The metaphors almost function with their own perichoresis.

Could we overlay the theological virtues on top of these? Within us dwells *charity,* which animates the heart with love for God and love for neighbor; it is one love with two objects. From above shines a light

---

28 Gregory the Great, *Moralia in Job,* vol. 3 (n.p.: Ex Fontibus, 2012), 32.
29 Gregory the Great, *Moralia in Job,* vol. 2 (n.p.: Ex Fontibus, 2012), 58.
30 Gregory the Great, *Moralia in Job,* 3:283.

by which *faith* sees the world; it is the Taboric light that shines from the altar at every eighth day. And now, already, *hope* waits patiently. It can do so because, as Péguy said, the little sister has already tasted the sweetness of heaven. By charity, faith, and hope, Christ directs our *inward* lives to truths *above* that will *one day* be completed. I don't think Gregory had these theological virtues in mind, but whenever we come across a triad, the resourceful theological mind can see connections. We go deep, we ascend, we await; we live from love, we live with faithful vision, we live in eager and hopeful anticipation. We are thrice born. We are born once, biologically; we await our final birth, eschatologically; we are reborn already, sacramentally. This is our liturgical mystical life stretching across, atop, along our temporal biological life, and it is the ordinarily miraculous life into which every Christian is plunged, not just the extraordinary mystics.

Nicholas Cabasilas offers a very interesting link between the three metaphors when he compares our first birth with our final birth. What happens to the saint on his rebirth is like what happens in the womb at the first birth. While the fetus is still in its dark and fluid life, nature prepares it "for that life which is in the light, and shapes it, as though according to a model, for the life which it is about to receive, [and] so likewise it happens to the saints."[31] Just as the saint does not understand why the theological virtues are being developed by liturgical asceticism, neither does the fetus understand why his body is developing as it is. We can imagine the fetus thinking: *Why do these bones in my legs continue to grow when they only cramp up the limited space I have? What are they for? They are of no use to me here, in this place. Why this nose when there is nothing to smell, these eyes when it is totally dark, these lungs that are ill-suited to this liquid environment? It is a waste to be developing these when they are of no use to me in my present life, in my present condition.* But having made the comparison, Cabasilas points out an important way in which the baby in the womb is different from saints-in-the-making:

> While the unborn have no perception whatever of this life, the blessed ones have many hints in this present life of things to come. . . . The unborn do not yet possess this life, but it is wholly in the future. In that condition there is no ray of light

---

[31] Nicholas Cabasilas, *The Life in Christ* (Crestwood, NY: St. Vladimir's Seminary Press, 1974), 44.

nor anything else which sustains this life. In our case this is not so, but that future light is, as it were, infused into this present life and mingled with it. . . . In this present world, therefore, it is possible for the saints not only to be disposed and prepared for that life, but also even now to live and act in accordance with it.[32]

Some faculties that have been forming in us since baptism, our other dark and fluid home, may also seem like they are growing to no purpose because we do not use them as we should, we are clumsy and inept in how we wield the theological virtues we have been given. Yet, they are growing in us for the day when we will need them.

Because the ending of the plotline has already been shown in Revelation, Cabasilas says we fetal saints do have some perception, even now in this life, of what is yet to come. The purpose of Revelation is to give a glimpse of the upcoming theosis, accomplished in the formative Torah, the presaging prophets, the revelation in the flesh in Bethlehem's cave, and the revelation in death and life outside Jerusalem's city limits. Only after we have seen the flower can we understand the seed; the omega is required to understand the alpha; until we see the tulip, the bulb looks like a gnarled knob. Until we run, we do not know what legs are for. The Son of God made flesh is required to understand the predestination of men and women.

Liturgy is the active presence *now* of an eschatological reality; liturgy is the kenosis of the transcendent Creator *within* his cosmos; and liturgy is the activity *below* of heaven above, the presence in the mundane of supernatural things. This is why the mysticism of our present life on earth is liturgical in nature. The blessed ones have things yet to come infused into their present life and mingled with their faith, hope, and love. They wait, but they see. They struggle, but they love. They perish, but they trust. The mystery of Christ is inscribed upon them in baptism, and they carry it on their brow. The theological virtues are poured into them as the consecrated water spills over the lip of the ecclesial font.

Ephrem the Syrian describes the economy of salvation by the metaphor of being reclothed in glory, which Sebastian Brock summarizes as having been doffed in the Fall and donned in the Incarnation, baptism, and resurrection:

---

[32] Cabasilas, *The Life in Christ*, 44–45.

At the Fall, Adam and Eve lose the "Robe of Glory" with which they had originally been clothed in Paradise; in order to re-clothe the naked Adam and Eve (in other words, humanity), God himself "puts on the body" from Mary, and at the Baptism Christ laid the Robe of Glory in the river Jordan, making it available once again for humanity to put on at baptism; then, at his or her baptism, the individual Christian, in "putting on Christ," puts on the Robe of Glory, thus re-entering the terrestrial anticipation of the eschatological Paradise, in other words, the Church; finally, at the Resurrection of the Dead, the just will in all reality re-enter the celestial Paradise, clothed in their Robes of Glory.[33]

The doffing of sin and donning of glory is liturgical mysticism practiced by the faithful members of the body of Christ in their sacramental life. Mysticism clothes us in supernatural light, but its cloth has been knitted by the Divine Weaver and fitted on our bodies in liturgical anticipation. When Jesus dove beneath the Jordan, he defeated Leviathan, compelled Adam's release, readjusted Eve's appetite, stripped Hades bare, invested waters with fecundate power, impregnated the womb of the Church, and joined Spirit to water so she could give birth to baby anointed ones (Christs). Every font is now charged with spiritual fire, and from every chalice we now drink sacramental blood. Adam mutinously ate from a tree and its fruit killed him; we meekly eat from the tree of the cross, and its fruitful flesh restores our life.

Christ seeks out Adam and Eve in his Paschal mystery. In Genesis 3 they hid themselves, naked and afraid, thinking themselves exempt from God, but what they thought a safe house turned out to be the doorway of a diabolical tunnel to Hades, which is where Christ had to go to find them, as the icons of the resurrection show. Sympathy with his Father's heart and obedience to his Father's will impel him to love man and woman and drive him to any lengths to make possible their arrival at the end for which they were created. It is a liturgical end. The Paschal mystery is a liturgical mystery. All the actions that Christ performed historically in his flesh and that he now continues celestially in his High Priesthood are done so that we can join him,

---

[33] Ephrem, *Hymns on Paradise*, introduction by Sebastian Brock (Crestwood, NY: St. Vladimir's Seminary Press, 1990), 67.

our brother, in his liturgy to the Father. The twin purposes of liturgy are the sanctification of man and the glorification of God, and these are exactly the purposes that constitute the mission of Christ. He came to glorify his Father by sanctifying his brothers. Liturgy is the perichoresis of the Trinity reaching out to us through the kenosis of the Son in order to invite our synergistic ascent to deification. That is the substance that occurs in all our ritual liturgies—from the Divine Liturgy on the eighth day, to the sacramental liturgies that initiate and heal and minister in love, to the liturgies of time observed during one revolution of the earth around the sun or during one rotation of the earth. Liturgy, then, is not one more cult of the Old Adam added to the world's stockpile, it is the cult of the New Adam perpetuated in a people animated by the Holy Spirit to perform Christ's liturgy, the liturgy of the New Adam. That is why we should think of our ecclesial activity as liturgical mysticism.

The mysticism is liturgical because it is the application of Christ's mysteries to our life. Louis Bouyer says this distinguishes Christian liturgical mysticism from all other types of mysticism. "What are called the non-Christian mysticisms can be confused with the mysticism of Christianity only so long as one continues stubbornly and against all common sense to eliminate from the mystical experience what–and, above all, the Person Who–is experienced."[34] This Person comes to us in liturgy. Christ comes to us in the *hierarchical liturgy* that flows from the heavenly throne to the Church's rites and sacraments, and he comes to us in the *mystical liturgy* that flows from the same throne to our personal reality saturated with that sacramental grace. Hierarchical liturgy is the perichoresis of the Trinity circulating in the Church, which is how Bouyer understands hierarchy: it is "the Divine Life's means of communication and circulation in the whole body."[35] *Visible liturgy* occurs as the activity of a visible hierarchy, authorized by Christ when he handed the priesthood to his apostles. *Invisible liturgy* occurs in every Christian soul when it responds to its gracing. And the purpose of the former is to bring the blood flow to every cell in the whole body. Invisible divine life is extended to us through sacraments designed to hallow us and bring our invisible,

---

[34] Louis Bouyer, *Introduction to Spirituality* (Notre Dame, IN: Christian Classics, 2013), 377.
[35] Louis Bouyer, *The Church Of God: Body of Christ and Temple of the Spirit* (San Francisco: Ignatius Press, 2011), 437.

mystical liturgy to perfection. The objective of the visible liturgy is to make our mystical glorification of God complete.

All of this mystery is liturgically founded, and all of our liturgy bears mystical fruit. The liturgist is a mystic, and the mystic is a liturgist. The mystic is a liturgical person who can speak with the mouth of the Son, see with the eyes of the Dove, join the Son's fellowship with the Father, see Jesus with the eyes of the Father, and have the Holy Spirit groaning within (Rom 8:26–27).

More than a river coming down from heaven, the whole city comes down from heaven, and liturgical mysticism is our residency in it. We are already citizens of the heavenly Jerusalem, only awaiting its completeness at the end of history. "Mystical experience is an experimental awareness of God which by means of the mysteries of faith, is given to the Christian who has the theological virtues, made supple by the gift of the Holy Ghost, in full measure."[36] The quickened faith of a baptized convert who has received the seed of eternal life will feel the need of being daily more deeply penetrated by the value of the Mass. If liturgy is our ascent to join Christ, the resurrected human high priest, then mysticism is standing beside him on the spiritual platform he has constructed for us in the perichoresis of the Trinity. Exterior, sacramental liturgy brings power to interior, personal liturgy; interior, personal liturgy brings life to exterior, sacramental liturgy. Let our mystical life rise up before God as incense. Liturgical asceticism makes us into granules of mystical incense to burn in glorification before God, and mysticism perfects our liturgy.

---

[36] A. Ple, "Mysticism and Mystery," ch. 1, in *Mystery and Mysticism* (London: Black Fryer's, 1956), 15.

CHAPTER 3

QUICKENING THE LITURGICAL PERSON

JUAN ARINTERO WRITES, "Even in its strictest signification or most characteristic state the mystical life is undoubtedly nothing but the complete manifestation of the Christian life or, rather, the development of the graces received in baptism."[1] The marred image of God is refreshed in baptism, but we are not complete until we grow into the full likeness of God. Final fullness awaits the eschaton, but the Christian mystical life is making progress toward it even now, even here. Baptism is a sacrament of initiation, therefore we should ask, "What does it initiate?" Jordan Aumann answers,

> Complete Christian perfection is found only in the mystical state. This is another conclusion that follows from the theological principles we have already established. Christian perfection consists in the full development of the sanctifying grace received at baptism as a seed. This development is verified by the increase of the infused theological and moral virtues, and especially that of charity, the virtue whose perfection coincides with the perfection of the Christian life.[2]

---

[1] John Arintero, *The Mystical Evolution In the Development and Vitality of the Church*, vol. 2 (Rockford, IL: Tan Books, 1978), 404.
[2] Jordan Aumann, *Spiritual Theology* (New York: Bloomsbury Continuum, 2018), 133.

Life in Christ, life in his mystical body, comes at a cost to our self-love (more on that in the next chapter), so the infused theological virtues initiate a spiritual warfare. We receive faith, hope, and charity in the regenerative waters, but once we have these theological gifts, we must still grow into them. Or, rather, they must grow more lively in us. To borrow an old English term, our baptism must be *quickened*.

That word has regrettably been restricted in modern English to mean not much more than a sense of acceleration. Even that narrowed meaning of the word is not useless, though, since we want to know how to accelerate our pace toward heaven. However, the original meanings were more complex and manifold. *Quick* means living (the quick of the fingernails), and we know it to refer to living persons from an old translation of the Apostle's Creed stating that God will come to "judge the quick and the dead." To "cut to the quick" means cutting through dead layers to living, sensitive tissue. *Quickening*, then, means to give additional life, to make something more lively and active. To *quicken* is to give life to, to animate, to make alive, to revive; to *be quickened* is to come back to life, to receive life, to take on a state of activity and vigor. To move more *quickly* is to move in a more *quickened* manner, and if we walk to heaven *quickly*, it is not only rapidly, but with a faith that is animated, lively, and bright. In pregnancy terms, *quickening* is the moment when the woman starts to feel movements in the womb. Mother Church is *quickened* when she starts to feel movements of faith in one of her children, and that child is *quickened* when he or she feels the sensation of eternal life stirring within. This is a liturgical anticipation of eschaton, which is why the Catechism defines faith as something that "makes us taste in advance the light of the beatific vision" (163). We await the day of our final birth in beatitude, but baptism has already planted a seed of glory, and liturgical mysticism is this seed *quickening*. We taste this light in sacramental liturgy and it matures into mystical experience when *quickened*, enlivened, brightened.

Liturgical mysticism is ecclesial in form and sacramental in nature. It does not leave the Church behind, or run alongside the Church, or transcend the Church by taking extra-ecclesial routes to heaven. It is not antihierarchical, anticlerical, anti-institutional, or antisocial (anti-ecclesial). Liturgical mysticism is a liturgical life that sprouts from baptism and seeks union with God through his mysteries, on a mystical level. Liturgical mysticism is the consummation of baptism like the adult is the consummation of the child, fruit is the consummation of flowering, sex is the consummation of the nuptial. Liturgical mysticism is what baptism will grow into if we willfully allow and personally abet it. Liturgy wells up from the deeps of baptism and now floats on the waters where Christ has put it for us to find. Cyril of Jerusalem tells his catechumens that it is right to call them Christs (plural, not possessive) because they "have become anointed ones by receiving the sign of the Holy Spirit"; and just as the Holy Spirit visited Christ when he came out of the Jordan, so they "emerged from the pool of sacred waters [and] were anointed in a manner corresponding with Christ's anointing."[3] This is where we find the Holy Spirit, who is source for all our spirituality. When Christ bathed in the river he invested the waters with his divine presence, and like an oil slick will float downstream, grace floats downstream from the Jordan to every baptismal font, wherever they are found in the world. Baptism creates a liturgical person, and liturgical mysticism quickens the life of that liturgical person.

Though it might seem peculiar to mix canon law with mysticism, the Code contains a definition of "person" that might be helpful. Canon 96 reads, "By baptism one is incorporated into the Church of Christ and is constituted a person in it with duties and rights which are proper to Christians."[4] Apparently, Christian persons are made, not born (Tertullian). Apparently, a Christian person is constructed, constituted, and composed in baptism. Behind this understanding is the ancient Roman definition of a person. To be a person in Rome was to have rights and duties; to receive rights and duties was to be made a person; to have no rights or duties meant that one was not a person, as was the case with slaves. So a commentary on this canon observes,

> The language of this opening canon therefore suggests the dual effect of baptism: it incorporates a human being into the Church of Christ, and it bestows a personhood upon him or her. The two are correlative. A person is classically understood—and so defined in this canon—as a subject of rights and duties. Incorporation into the larger community then

---

[3] Cyril of Jerusalem, Sermon 3.1, in *The Awe-Inspiring Rites of Initiation: The Origins of the RCIA*, ed. Edward Yarnold, S.J. (Collegeville: The Liturgical Press, 1994), 81.

[4] *The Code of Canon Law: A Text and Commentary, Study Edition*, commissioned by The Canon Law Society of America, ed. J. Coriden, T. Green, and D. Heintschel (New York: Paulist Press, 1985), 70.

fixes these rights and duties . . . within the individual physical person. The portal is baptism—and since the Church is the visible communion . . . the external sacramental act of affiliation must also be a visible, perceptible one, i.e., baptism of water.[5]

Liturgical mysticism is *personal* insofar as it is the mystery of Trinitarian love being reproduced in a person's soul, and the soul of a liturgical person receives personhood from the *corporate*, sacramental body acting as an instrument of Christ. There is no friction or opposition between corporate and personal, between sacramental liturgy and personal liturgy (liturgy that goes on in a person's life). The former makes the latter possible, the latter makes the former *quicker*. Because the liturgical act of baptism has created a person with rights and duties in the Church, there follows liturgical mysticism. Liturgy is the perichoresis of the Trinity kenotically extending itself—this time into an individual's life to reecho and reproduce its mystery of love in that person. Paul Evdokimov writes,

> A saint is not a superman, but one who discovers and lives his truth as a liturgical being. The best definition of a human being comes from the liturgy. The true man or woman is one who proclaims the Trisagion and the Sanctus. . . . It is not enough to say prayers, one must become, be prayer, prayer incarnate. It is not enough to have moments of praise. All of life, each act, every gesture, even the smile of the human face, must become a hymn of adoration, an offering, a prayer. One should offer not what one has, but what one is.[6]

Who is the liturgical person in the presence of divine reality? Everything we need to say about theological anthropology is contained in two affirmations: (i) Man is made in the image of God; (ii) God is a Trinity. The one in whose image we are made is one whose being is communion. If the human image is to grow further into the divine likeness, the human person should grow into love's communion in greater and greater degree, *quickly*. Philosophers have spilled ink over

---

5   *The Code of Canon Law*, 71.

6   Paul Evdokimov, *The Art of the Icon: A Theology of Beauty* (Redondo Beach, CA: Oakwood, 1990), 15.

defining "human being," as distinct from "natural being" and "animal being," but have rarely given adequate attention to the communion-basis of the person that liturgical mysticism assumes. The Old Testament can help because the Hebrews did not think except in relational terms. A person can neither bring himself into existence, nor keep himself there, and therefore when Israel thought about man and woman as image of God, they thought in terms of a dependent relationship. To say "I am *imago Dei*" is like saying "I am husband": the noun describing my identity comes from a relationship-verb. When Gabriel Marcel was trying to overcome a dualism in how we think of body and soul, he observed that we're fooled by our language. When we say, "I have a body," we're fooled into thinking there's an "I" and a "body" and our job is somehow to connect them. We make some advance by saying, "I am a body," but that still assumes two things, this time connected not possessively but at the level of two juxtaposed ontologies. So Marcel's final recommendation is "I am bodily." The way I am is bodily. In a similar vein, we don't want to say, "I have an image of God," or even "I am in the image of God," we want to say, "I am as *imago Dei*." But for being *imago Dei*, I would not be. I exist as a term of a relationship. I don't "have" relationships; I am, relationally. This is an image of Trinitarian perichoresis.

A theologian of the Old Testament, Gerhard von Rad, offers an explanation about the meaning of the Hebrew word we translate as "image":

> *Selem* means predominantly an actual plastic work, a duplicate, sometimes an idol. . . . We learn from a number of ancient Oriental myths that a god makes a man (or a god) in his image. . . . Just as powerful earthly kings, to indicate their claim to dominion, erect an image of themselves in the provinces of their empire where they don't personally appear, so man is placed upon earth in God's image as God's sovereign emblem. He is really only God's representative, summoned to maintain and enforce God's claim to dominion over the earth.[7]

---

[7] Gerhard von Rad, *Genesis, The Old Testament Library* (Philadelphia, Westminster Press, 1972), 57, 60.

Thus, when the Pharaoh Ramesses II wanted to indicate that he ruled a range of territory, he had his image hewn out of rock on the Mediterranean coast north of Beirut, and the presence of his image meant that he was the ruler of this area. So it is that man and woman are set in the midst of creation as God's *selem*, his statue or image. Yahweh is not only the ruler of the invisible ranks of angels and archangels, Yahweh is also ruler of material, visible creation, and the visible evidence of this is the presence of his image, man and woman. They stand as *imago Dei* at the center point of two relationships, stretching out in two directions. They are simultaneously *over* creation and *under* God: the first relationship stretches downward, as they have dominion over nature, but that dominion itself is conditioned by a second relationship that stretches upward, because they stand under the authority of another. Any power humanity possesses over creation is conditioned by a liturgical duty. We were created to be royal priests and must take care not to separate the one from the other, or our exercise of dominion will get out of hand. Any exercise of royalty is hand-in-glove with the exercise of priesthood.

Fr. Alexander Schmemann describes man's unique role by calling men and women *homo adorans*—beings capable of giving adoration.

> All rational, spiritual and other qualities of man, distinguishing him from other creatures, have their focus and ultimate fulfillment in this capacity to bless God, to know, so to speak, the meaning of the thirst and hunger that constitutes his life. "*Homo sapiens*," "*homo faber*" . . . yes, but, first of all, "*homo adorans*." The first, the basic definition of man is that he is *the priest*. He stands in the center of the world and unifies it in his act of blessing God, of both receiving the world from God and offering it to God. . . . The world was created as the "matter," the material of one all-embracing eucharist, and man was created as the priest of this cosmic sacrament.[8]

God makes a being after his own image, and such a being has dominion over matter in order to gather it up to serve the cosmic liturgy. Man and woman are the priestly tongue of mute creation.

Because grace perfects nature, and does not destroy it, deification

---

[8] Alexander Schmemann, *For the Life of the World* (Crestwood, NY: St. Vladimir's Seminary Press, 1973), 15.

perfects anthropology, and does not wreck it. The person who becomes a liturgical person is perfected by new rights and duties added in baptism to the rights and duties he possessed as a natural person. Adam and Eve were cosmic priests as they exercised their dominion in the Garden; the sons and daughters of the New Adam, born from the New Eve, now exercise Christ's priesthood. Of all the descendants of Adam and Eve, none is greater than John the Baptist, yet the priesthood of one who is least in the Kingdom of God is greater than his (Luke 7:28). In their liturgical mysticism, the baptized royal priest makes connection of this material world with a greater spiritual universe, as described by Louis Bouyer:

> The tradition of the Fathers has never admitted the existence of a material world apart from a larger creation, from a spiritual universe. To speak more precisely, for them the world, a whole and a unity, is inseparably matter and spirit. What we call the material world is only the reflection of a reflection. . . . It is, as it were, the fringe of their garment: the waves of its light are like the scintillating robe with which the Creator has been pleased to adorn his invisible creation.
>
> Across this continuous chain of creation, in which the triune fellowship of the divine persons has, as it were, extended and propagated itself, moves the ebb and flow of the creating *Agape* and of the created *eucharistia*.[9]

Bouyer imagines it as "an infinitely generous heart, beating with an unceasing diastole and systole, first diffusing the divine glory in paternal love, then continually gathering it up again to its immutable source in filial love."[10] The liturgical mystic lives by the rhythm of this heartbeat. God's love flows downward, creating as it goes. Creation's thanksgiving flows back upward, giving latria as it goes. At the center point stands the liturgical mystic, receiving agape and returning eucharistia in his and her unique anthropological capacity now perfected in mystical priesthood.

We do not await deliverance from the body, we await the resurrection of the whole person that will involve the body, and any mystical

---

9   Louis Bouyer, *The Meaning of the Monastic Life* (London: Burnes & Oates, 1955), 28.
10   Bouyer, *The Meaning of the Monastic Life*, 28.

elevations that are Christian will not be to the detriment or derogation of our physical reality. The scholastic theologians went to great lengths to speak always with a Hebraic sense of the interconnection between body and soul. The scholastic slogan was *anima forma corporis* (the soul is the life form of the body). Etienne Gilson makes the point memorably when he says, "For St. Thomas, following Aristotle, the soul does not first make a body move, it first makes it a body. A corpse is not a body. The soul makes it exist as a body."[11] The soul in-forms the body. We are, bodily. The soul animates the body, and when it stops doing so the person is dead. That is why Anscar Vonier says, "By soul, Catholic philosophy understands a principle of life and sensation for the body," but what makes the human soul different from the animal soul is that the highest part of the human soul has spirit-functions, too, because "the human soul is a spirit. . . . [T]he human soul is as much a spirit as God Himself, as much a spirit as any of the Angels of God."[12] And since the soul is the life form of the body, the Catechism can say, "The human body shares in the dignity of 'the image of God': it is a human body precisely because it is animated by a spiritual soul, and it is the whole person that is intended to become, in the body of Christ, a temple of the Spirit [Cf. *1 Cor* 6:19–20; 15:44–45]" (CCC 364). Mysticism that is liturgical will involve matter and bodies.

If mysticism is ascent higher and higher into God, the Christian mystic additionally understands he is ascending further and further into community, since God is a community of love. The soul may feel alone during its purging, but it is never purged in order to be left alone. What awaits in heaven is a choir, a city, an army, a *communio sanctorum* with a Trinity at its head. Liturgical mysticism is not cold, it is saintly; it is not indifferent, it is charitable; it is not private, it is ecclesial; it is not egocentric, it is hierarchical. Deification is traffic on the ladder of Dionysian hierarchy.

The goal of a hierarchy, then, is to enable beings to be as like as possible to God and to be at one with him. . . . Hierarchy causes its members to be images of God in all respects, to be clear and spotless mirrors reflecting the glow of primordial light and indeed of God himself. . . . Indeed for every mem-

---

[11] Etienne Gilson, *The Christian Philosophy of St. Thomas Aquinas* (Notre Dame: University of Notre Dame Press, 1956), 187.
[12] Anscar Vonier, *The Human Soul* (London: B. Herder, 1913), 1.

ber of the hierarchy, perfection consists in this, that it is up-
lifted to imitate God as far as possible and, more wonderful
still, that it becomes what scripture calls a fellow workman
for God.[13]

The Father reaches out and grabs hold of us by the Son and Holy Spirit to bring us to completion, to reap the image sown when it bears the
fruit of likeness. Though the idea of image and likeness is sometimes
considered more Byzantine than Latin, the Catechism of the Catholic
Church uses it to summarize the reason for all of salvation history:
"Disfigured by sin and death, man remains 'in the image of God,' in
the image of the Son, but is deprived 'of the glory of God' [*Rom* 3:23],
of his 'likeness.' The promise made to Abraham inaugurates the economy of salvation, at the culmination of which the Son himself will
assume that 'image' and restore it in the Father's 'likeness' by giving it
again its Glory, the Spirit who is 'the giver of life'" [CCC 705].

Many of the Fathers of the Church likened deification to putting
iron into fire. By itself, and of its own nature, iron is cold, but it glows
red hot in the fire, "by the grace" of the fire, so to speak. The iron does
not possess the heat of itself. If it is withdrawn it loses this quality,
but as long as it remains in the fire it enjoys heat as if it were its own.
When the Son assumed human nature, his divine nature deified the
human nature which he had assumed, and now our personal mystical
union with the God-man participates in his hypostatic union. This
whole idea is nicely expressed through iconographic images, as Bishop Schönborn demonstrates: "In our divine transformation, therefore,
there is at work a *synergism*, a cooperative action: grace confers the
divine seal, and practicing the virtues imprints on us the features of
God's image. . . . Man is capable of receiving this imprint, the features of the divine image, because the Son, through the union with
his human nature, has first impressed on it his sonship."[14] Liturgical
mysticism is growth in holiness, and the holiness which is *quickening* is simply our resemblance to Christ Jesus. According to Columba
Marmion, the reason for everything God has done is to bring about

---

[13] Dionysius, *The Celestial Hierarchy*, ch. 3, in *Pseudo-Dionysius, the Complete Works*,
trans. Colm Luibheid, The Classics of Western Spirituality (New York: Paulist
Press, 1987), 153–154.

[14] Christoph Schonborn, *God's Human Face: The Christ-Icon* (San Francisco: Ignatius
Press, 1994), 101.

this resemblance. "The wonderful mysteries of the incarnation, the Passion, the Resurrection, and the triumph of Jesus, the institution of the Church and the Sacraments, grace, the virtues, the gifts of the Holy Spirit, all this marvelous supernatural order has come forth from this movement of the Heart of God so as to make us His children."[15]

Christian mysticism has always been understood to be in, with, and through Christ (as we say at every Mass), and Emile Mersch establishes how important this is to Paul by observing that the apostle uses the phrase *en Christo* 164 times in his writings. Examples are easy to think of. "So you also must consider yourselves dead to sin and alive to God in Christ Jesus" (Rom 6:11). "There is therefore now no condemnation for those who are in Christ Jesus" (Rom 8:1). He tells the Ephesians they are "created in Christ Jesus for good works" (Eph 2:10), and the Galatians that "in Christ Jesus" they are sons of God through faith (Gal 3:26), and the Philippians that they should have in them the mind which is theirs "in Christ Jesus" (Phil 2:5). The Christian's union with Christ is more than a historical union, like we have with George Washington; it is more than a philosophical union, like we have with Socrates; it is more than an imaginative union, like we have with Aslan; it is more than an idealistic union, like we have with fellow members of our club. This is a mystical and sacramental union. Both the Church and the Christian must be understood mystically and sacramentally because sacramental liturgy and personal, mystical liturgy are united.

Theological vocabulary has worked this out with some concise terminology that distinguishes "moral union" from "physical union." We can borrow an explanation from Matthias Scheeben's book *Nature and Grace*, where he peels back the layers of meaning in the Greek word we want to understand. *Physis* has a background meaning of "birth" (it means begetting something); so it can mean the begetting principle itself, or power that can beget; or it can signify what the begetter communicates by generation (a puppy has the same physis as the dog that gave it birth); therefore physis denotes the essential, vital form being communicated (this is metaphysical form, not "shape," and refers to what makes the thing what it is); and finally, it can mean the principle of motion which makes the thing act like the thing it

---

[15] Columba Marmion, *Christ: The Ideal of the Monk* (London & Edinburgh: Sands; and St. Louis: Herder, 1922), 224–225.

is.[16] Physis has to do with essences and powers and vital forms. Therefore the philosophers made a distinction between two kinds of union. A "moral union" comes from one thing exerting influence on the other and means no more than the development of the natural powers a being already has. A "physical union" (i.e., a union at the level of physis) means the powers of X are found in Y. "As is evident, the word [physis] primarily and mainly signifies the form, the determining and moving principle in composite beings,"[17] which occurs not when a new direction is imparted to existing powers, but when "new, higher powers are infused which raised the entire organism of nature to a higher plane and make it capable of wholly new kind of activity."[18] The supernatural imparts a vital power, a new capacity, and an inclination to move, a new *habitus*. "The habit we are speaking of is not acquired by repeated acts, but is divinely infused. St. Thomas well-defined the nature of the supernatural principle of life when he teaches that it is a state by which the soul enters into such a relation with a higher nature as to share in its life."[19] When a monk takes his vows he receives his habit; this has described the baptismal habit in which all liturgists dress.

Christ does not simply have a moral union with the members of his "Jesus club," he has a union with members of his mystical body by which they participate in Christ's energies, which he shares with us, drawing from intimate communion with his Father in heaven. He is a hypostatic union (union at the level of person) of divine nature and human nature, and whereas he is in union with God as the only-begotten Son, and whereas he is in union with us as a fellow human being, he mediates our union with the Father. We are adopted to also become sons of God in a filial relationship that both men and women have when they join a new race on earth, called the Church. "His divine power has granted to us all things that pertain to life and godliness, through the knowledge of him who called us to his own glory and excellence, by which he has granted to us his precious and very great promises, that through these you may escape from the corruption that is in the world because of passion, and become partakers of the divine nature" (2 Pet 1:3–4). The union is brought about by

---

[16] Matthias Scheeben, *Nature and Grace* (St. Louis: B. Herder, 1954), 20–21.

[17] Scheeben, *Nature and Grace*, 21.

[18] Scheeben, *Nature and Grace*, 38.

[19] Scheeben, *Nature and Grace*, 154, citing Thomas at *ST* IIae, q. 110, a. 4.

an imitation that is sacramental of a death that is real, says Cyril of Alexandria.

> What a wonder and a paradox! We have not actually died, we have not really been buried, when we have not, in reality, after having been crucified, risen again. But the imitation is effected in an image (*en eikoni*), salvation in reality (*en aletheia*). Christ was really crucified, really placed in the tomb; He really rose again. And all these things were done through love for us, so that, sharing by imitation in his sufferings, we might truly obtain salvation. . . . He has given me the grace of salvation without my having suffered or struggled.[20]

This union is initiated upon baptism into the Son of God, confirmed with an anointing in the Holy Spirit, and quickened across a lifetime of mystical growth.

Liturgical mysticism is becoming by grace what Christ is by nature. St. Paul reminds the baptized Christians that they have clothed themselves with Christ (Gal 3:27), and when John Chrysostom preached on that text he says, "If Jesus Christ is the Son of God, and if you have put Him on, having the Son in you and being assimilated to him, you have been raised to one and the same relation, one and the same form . . . you are all in Christ Jesus; that is to say, you only have one form, one figure, that of Jesus Christ."[21] Our liturgical unity with Christ received through the sacrament penetrates into our personal liturgy practiced as mysticism. Connecting "physis" with its Latin translation as *natura*, we can make sense of 2 Peter 1:4 referring to "partakers of the divine nature" (*theias koinonoi physeos*), and Romans 6:5 referring to being "united with him (*sumphutoi*) in a death like his," and Gregory of Nyssa referring to the Eucharist as containing a body made immortal that acts like a leaven: "Just as a little leaven . . . is assimilated into all the dough, so the body made immortal by God, once having entered into ours, transforms it and changes it completely into itself, . . . into its own nature" (*pros ton eautou physin*).[22]

---

[20] Cyril of Jerusalem, in Jean Daniélou, *The Bible and the Liturgy* (Notre Dame, IN: University of Notre Dame Press, 1966), 44.

[21] John Chrysostom, Commentary on Galatians 3.5, taken from Jules Gross, *The Divinization of the Christian According to the Greek Fathers* (Anaheim, CA: A&C Press, 2002), 204.

[22] Gregory Nyssa, *Oratio Catechetica* 37, in Jules Gross, *The Divinization*, 185.

The graces received should also make us love as Christ loved, love with Christ's power, which is why John Chrysostom says nothing is better suited to prolonging the effects of the Eucharist than a visit paid to Christ in his little ones. The poor standing in the public square remind Chrysostom of the majesty of an altar made ready for sacrifice. The poor are an altar on which we can make our sacrifice of almsgiving, so he compares them to the stone altar in the Church by saying they are the living altar.

> This altar [of the poor] is composed of the very members of Christ, and the Lord's body becomes an altar for thee. Venerate it; for upon it, in the flesh, thou dost offer sacrifice to the Lord. This altar is greater than the altar in his church. . . . Do not protest! The *stone* altar is august because of the Victim that rests upon it; but the *altar of almsgiving* is more so because it is made of this very Victim. This altar you can see everywhere, in the streets and in the market place, and at any hour you may offer sacrifice thereon; for it too is a place of sacrifice. And, as the priest standing at the altar brings down the Spirit, so you too bring down the Spirit, like the oil which was poured out in abundance. [23]

What generosity by God! He provides us an altar for sacrifice wherever we are. The poor await us anywhere, everywhere. The liturgical mystics we meet in the history of the Church are ravished with love for the poor.

If we are in communion with Christ, then his activity can be found in us. And what was the one, central, overriding activity of Jesus? To glorify the Father and, by means of the Spirit, to bring all things before the Father. This I propose as a definition of "mystical sacrifice." Augustine says sacrifice is "every action done so as to cling to God in communion of holiness, and thus achieve blessedness."[24] This can serve as a description of Christ's whole life—to cling to God in communion of holiness and receive his blessing. His death on the cross was only the exterior climax of an interior sacrificial life. Li-

---

[23] John Chrysostom, *Homily 20 on II Corinthians*, quoted in Emile Mersch, *The Whole Christ: The Historical Development of the Doctrine of the Mystical Body in Scripture and Tradition*, trans. John R. Kelly (Milwaukee: Bruce, 1938), 335.

[24] The Catechism has made his definition its own at *CCC* 2099.

turgical mysticism takes nourishment from Christ, and that involves bringing ourselves into a state of unity with his sacrificial existence. In his book on the Eucharist, Raniero Cantalamessa wants to know how it is that the cross is not ended and concluded, like every other event in history.[25] Every other historical event disappears into the past after its fruition, and we do not have the power to conjure up again any event out of history, we can only remember it. Yet the cross is a continuing presence to us, and to the Father. How is this possible? Cantalamessa's answer is pneumatological. The event of the cross is a spiritual event because of the Holy Spirit; the cross is an eternal event because this is the eternal Spirit; the Paschal mystery is present mystically because what is done in the Spirit will never fade from sight or significance.

The relationship of Son and Spirit in the Gospel has already revealed how they work in collaboration—like the two hands of the Father, Irenaeus said.[26] The Son is conceived by the power of the Holy Spirit (Matt 1:18); the Spirit descends on him at the Jordan (Matt 3:16); he is led by this Spirit into the desert for forty days of ascetical battle with Satan (Matt 4:1); after those forty days, he comes back to Galilee in the power of the Spirit (Luke 4:14); the Spirit anoints him so he could preach the good news (Luke 4:18); he is the servant who is God's delight, about whom the prophet said God's Spirit would be poured (Matt 12:18); he drives out demons by means of the Spirit (Matt 12:28); when he praises the Father he does so rejoicing in the Spirit (Luke 10:21); he will baptize with this Spirit while John only baptized with water (Mark 18); a blasphemy against this Spirit will not be forgiven (Mark 3:29); at trial his disciples needn't worry because it will not be them speaking but this Spirit (Mark 13:11); he tells Nicodemus that he has to be born of water and the Spirit (John 3:5); the one sent by God is given the Spirit without limit (John 3:34); his disciples will only understand his words without grumbling and offense if the Spirit gives them life (John 6:63); when he promises streams of living water given to those who thirst, he meant the Spirit, who would be given when he was glorified (John 7:39). Jesus lived a

---

[25] Raniero Cantalamessa, *The Eucharist: Our Sanctification* (Collegeville, MN: Liturgical Press, 1995), 13.

[26] Irenaeus, *Against Heresies* 5.6, in *The Ante-Nicene Fathers*, vol. 1, *The Apostolic Fathers, Justin Martyr, Irenaeus*, ed. Alexander Roberts and James Donaldson (Peabody, Massachusetts: Hendrickson, 2004), 531.

spiritual life! The Letter to the Hebrews says that Christ offered himself without blemish to God through the eternal Spirit (Heb 9:14), and Cantalamessa concludes that "these words shed new light on the event of the Cross; it appears as a 'spiritual' event, as the work of the Holy Spirit."[27] The life of Christ was permeated by the Spirit. So was his death. And so is his resurrected life—in us, now. The same work that the Holy Spirit did over him, he will do over us. The Spirit will include us in the same work that Christ is presently performing. The sacrifice of the Mass is a spiritual event because it is a work of the Holy Spirit.

And here is how Cantalamessa describes that spiritual sacrifice. "At every 'breaking of the bread' when the priest breaks the host, it's as if the alabaster vase of Christ's humanity were being broken again, which is what happened on the Cross, and as if the perfume of his obedience were rising to touch the Father's heart again."[28] Christ drops himself into his Church and his aroma permeates each member. Paul writes, "For we are the aroma of Christ to God among those who are being saved and among those who are perishing, to one a fragrance from death to death, to the other a fragrance from life to life" (2 Cor 2:15–16). The liturgical mystic is the good odor of Christ, the sacrificed Lamb of God whose blood is poured upon us to extinguish the smell of death.

This mystical-physical union is not only a matter of us calling out to Christ, but of him calling out to us. He desires union with us, too. Our deification is not only our goal, it is God's goal as well. There is nothing Christ wishes with more intensity and enthusiasm than to have us step up into divine life. There is nothing Christ desires more than a liturgical mystic. His aching is also expressed in the Eucharist, and who better to enunciate it than the golden-mouthed preacher, John Chrysostom, who places the following words into the mouth of Christ speaking to a communicant approaching the altar. Here, the kenosis becomes personal.

> For thee I was covered with blows and spittle; I divested Myself of My glory, I left My Father and I came to thee, to thee who didst hate me, who didst flee Me, who didst not wish even to hear My name. I followed thee, I ran after thee: I

27 Cantalamessa, *The Eucharist*, 14.
28 Cantalamessa, *The Eucharist*, 13.

caught hold of thee and embraced thee. "Eat Me," I said, "and drink Me. . . . It is not enough that I should possess thy first fruits [the physical body of Christ] in heaven; that does not satisfy My love. I come once more to the earth, not only to 'mingle' myself with thee, but to entwine Myself in thee. I am eaten, I am broken into pieces, that this fusion, this union, may be more intimate. When other things are united, each remains distinct in itself; but I weave Myself into thee. I want nothing to come between us; I wish the two to become one."[29]

This is the sort of union possible only because it arises from the Incarnation and remains effective in liturgical sacrament.

Because liturgical mysticism concerns the anointing of our lives with Christ, and occurs over the course of our life in the holy ecclesia, I choose to consider mysticism as belonging to pastoral theology. This may sound peculiar to our ears if we think of mysticism as flying high in the heavens and pastoral work as drudging in the trenches. But I mean it seriously. Pastoral theology is the theology that shepherds souls to eternal life, which means nurturing the seeds of the mystical life planted in baptism. All shepherds of the Church should be leading their flock into mystical pastures where their sheep can feed more profoundly upon the bread from heaven. In his address at the beginning of the new millennium, John Paul II laid down the challenge of connecting pastoral ministry with holiness. "First of all, I have no hesitation in saying that all pastoral initiatives must be set in relation to *holiness*. . . . Stressing holiness remains more than ever an urgent pastoral task."[30] He continues by connecting holiness, pastoral ministry, and baptism.

What might the word 'holiness' mean in the context of a pastoral plan? In fact, to place pastoral planning under the heading of holiness is a choice filled with consequences. It implies the conviction that, since Baptism is a true entry into the holiness of God through incorporation into Christ and the indwelling of his Spirit, it would be a contradiction to settle for a life of mediocrity, marked by a minimalist ethic

---

[29] John Chrysostom, *Homily 15 on 1 Timothy 5:11–15*, in Emile Mersch, *The Whole Christ* (Milwaukee, WI: Bruce, 1938), 328.

[30] John Paul II, Apostolic Letter *Novo Millennio Ineunte* (January 6, 2001), §30.

and a shallow religiosity. To ask catechumens: "Do you wish to receive Baptism?" means at the same time to ask them: "Do you wish to become holy?" It means to set before them the radical nature of the Sermon on the Mount: "Be perfect as your heavenly Father is perfect" (Mt 5:48).[31]

Baptism is the reception of an ascetical discipline that is designed to lead to theologia, holiness, mystical union with God, if only we keep our baptism *quick* (alive). John Paul II indicates that rediscovering the Church as mystery is bound to bring with it a rediscovery of the Church's holiness. "To profess the Church is holy means to point to her as the Bride of Christ. . . . This as it were objective gift of holiness is offered to all the baptized. But the gift in turn becomes a task, which must shape the whole of Christian life: 'This is the will of God, your sanctification' (1 Thess 4:3). It is a duty which concerns not only certain Christians."[32]

Therefore, holiness involves pastoral ministry. When the substance of the liturgy becomes the substance of the soul of the pastor, then his ministry will become a pastoral anointing of the Mysteries of Christ that he is ordained to apply to souls. The liturgy is the sacramental moment of mysteries, but those mysteries are not confined to the moment. The reason we receive them in the sacraments is in order that they might come to life in us, *quicken* us, perfect us on our journey to our final end. It is unfortunate that we often think of the word "pastoral" like a sort of dilution, like putting too much water in the soup. Perhaps we could rehabilitate the term by its etymology. "Pastor," the noun, involves "pastoring," the verb. The pastor pastors; the shepherd shepherds. The pastor does *pascere,* meaning "to feed, to lead to pasture, cause to eat."[33] "[D]o you love me?" Jesus asked Peter repetitively (John 21:15–17). *Then lead my sheep to pasture, set them to graze, cause them to eat.* Eat what? Jesus himself. But "[h]ow can this man give us his flesh to eat?" (John 6:52). Jesus sits on a mystical throne, awaiting us at the mystical altar, and the pastor, as shepherd, brings his flock to Christ's liturgical location—not because Christ is confined on this altar, since the Logos moves freely throughout the

---

[31] John Paul II, *Novo Millennio Ineunte,* §31.

[32] John Paul II, *Novo Millennio Ineunte,* §30.

[33] Online Etymology Dictionary, s.v. "pastor (n.)," accessed April 11, 2019, https://www.chicagomanualofstyle.org/book/ed17/part3/ch14/psec233.html.

cosmos he created, but because here Christ's body and blood, soul and divinity is truly, really, and substantially present, and because here Christ the high priest is still performing his cult to the Father and integrates us into his sacrifice. The ascended Christ conducts his eternal priesthood at the altar in heaven, but there is a sacramental wormhole between that invisible altar and this visible one. (Definition of a wormhole: "A distortion of space-time that links one location or time with another, through a path that is shorter in distance or duration than would otherwise be expected."[34]) When Benedict XVI sees Paul coordinate a death on a cross with the cosmic liturgy and this cultic liturgy, he is amazed. Paul interprets "Christ's death on the cross in terms of the cult. . . . We are still hardly able to grasp the enormous importance of this step. An event that was in itself profane, the execution of a man by the most cruel and horrible method available, is described as a cosmic liturgy, as tearing open the closed-up heavens."[35] The visible liturgical altar is the sacramental pathway to the invisible altar, to the heavenly, beatific meadow where we will be finally pastured.[36]

I have used liturgical asceticism as a parallel for liturgical mysticism. Arintero said mystical life is the complete manifestation of the Christian life; Bouyer says something similar about the monastic ascetical life: "The monastic life is simply the perfect flowering of the Christian life. The monastery is simply the apex of the pilgrim Church. Or, if you prefer, it is the anticipated realization of its eternal destiny."[37] Likewise, the extraordinary mystic is an anticipated realization of the eternal destiny of each ordinary liturgical mystic. We may be appropriately inspired by mystics who receive extraordinary graces to serve as encouraging witnesses to us, just as we may be appropriately inspired by monks whose extraordinary asceticism inspires ours. But in both cases, the apex is attached to the liturgical base of the triangle. Mysticism rises up to heaven, but it rises out of

---

[34] *The American Heritage Dictionary of the English Language*, s.v. "wormhole," accessed April 11, 2019, https://ahdictionary.com/word/search.html?q=wormhole.

[35] Joseph Ratzinger, "Eucharist and Mission," in *Pilgrim Fellowship of Faith: The Church As Communion* (San Francisco: Ignatius Press, 2005), 94–95.

[36] This paragraph arose while preparing remarks for the Mullen lecture given at St. Mary Seminary & Graduate School of Theology in Cleveland, published as "The Pastoral Minister as Liturgical Pedagogue," in *Antiphon*, vol. 22, no. 3 (2018): 273–293.

[37] Bouyer, *The Meaning of the Monastic Life*, 37.

the Church, for the Church is the opportunity to live life in the new eon commenced by Christ's Paschal mystery. Being baptized by sacrament into his mystery makes our lives a personal liturgy rotating around the twin poles of glorifying God and cooperating with our sanctification. But this requires labor of us, which we should consider in the next chapter.

CHAPTER 4

THE NARROW GATE

BAPTISM DROPS THE SPIRIT OF THE HOLY ONE into our veins, but there is no fire where there is not matter to burn; asceticism is the cost of making us combustible, and that fire is a mystical one. Liturgy is ecstasy: going out of one's self to abide in God. But killing our self-love requires ascetical fortitude. Mysticism is not a character trait that only some people have, like blue eyes or a quick temper. Neither is mysticism a feat accomplished by our own abilities, like writing a novel or playing the trombone. Mysticism is caused by grace, and grace abides in the Church, which is communion in the Holy Spirit, by whose dominion one can develop a life that is spiritual, begun when baptism infuses the supernatural graces of faith, hope, and love. However, these gifts must be put to work in our hearts, and the sinner's heart initially resists.

The liturgical *habitus* infused by God through the sacramental water brings us face to face with the Paschal mystery in a regular and repetitive rhythm, if we are obedient disciples. We routinely step before God's throne whence the river of liturgy flows. And from the altar of the Lord we are sanctified, authorized by the Holy Spirit to join the Son's glorification of the Father, and then carried by this liturgical current back into the world to effect its consecration. It was in this context that Paul VI defined consecration as "the reestablishment of a thing's relationship to God according to its own order, according to the exigency of the nature of the thing itself, in the plan willed by

God."[1] With this liturgical capacity, we can use the world to glorify God, but it comes at the cost of being able to handle the world. Alas! We do not do nature naturally anymore, we do not do the world liturgically anymore, because the Fall was the forfeiture of our liturgical career. A perversion has entered the garden where Adam and Eve were to have exercised their cosmic priesthood, and it led them to repudiate their core identity as *homo adorans*. Satan seduced us into his rebellion and corrupted our relationship with God, the world, and each other. The world is good, but fallen. The world is God's gift, but we have "bent it," as C. S. Lewis states in *The Screwtape Letters*. Using this metaphor, the demon Screwtape reminds his nephew Wormwood that although Satan cannot create anything whatsoever, he can twist things:

> Never forget that when we are dealing with any pleasure in its healthy and normal and satisfying form, we are, in a sense, on the Enemy's ground. I know we have won many a soul through pleasure. All the same, it is [God's] invention, not ours. He made the pleasures: all our research so far has not enabled us to produce one. All we can do is to encourage the humans to take the pleasures which our Enemy has produced, at times, or in ways, or in degrees, which He has forbidden.
>
> He's vulgar, Wormwood. He has a bourgeois mind. He has filled His world full of pleasures. There are things for humans to do all day long without His minding in the least— sleeping, washing, eating, drinking, making love, playing, praying, working. Everything has to be twisted before it's any use to us. We fight under cruel disadvantages. Nothing is naturally on our side.[2]

It is certainly true that matter has not fallen—there is nothing wrong with money, sex, or beer; but the human heart has been corrupted— the problem is avarice, lust, and gluttony, passions that give us trouble when using material things properly. Satan can use good things as bait on his hooks of envy and pride and self-love. There could be no

---

[1] Paul VI, "Layman Should Be World's Perfect Citizen," Audience of May 1, 1969 (at http://www.ewtn.com/library/PAPALDOC/P6LAYMAN.HTM).

[2] C. S. Lewis, *Screwtape Letters*, in *The Complete C. S. Lewis Signature Classics* (San Francisco: HarperSanFrancisco, 2007), 210.

flaw in the material creation that would deform the world's hierarchical and iconic beauty, for God is the master of matter. But there could be, and was, a movement in the spiritual creation that could, and did, upset this beauty.

Bouyer describes Lucifer as one created to be Prince of this world, the morning star, a creature-servant in the hierarchy "on whom the last wave of light broke, the last echo of the great Eucharist resounded. . . . What happened then? What has intervened? Simply, pride."[3] He was an angel in the hierarchy whose appointed task was to pass agape downward from heaven above, and eucharistia upward from earth below, but he abandoned his post in the hierarchy. He became the first anarchist, the first to begrudge latria, the first anti-liturgist. He became the antichrist (rebelling against God's Kingdom), Satan (the tempter), the devil (slanderer), diabolical (*dia-baleo*, to throw apart), as he and his followers formed "a screen against the spontaneous movement of response which was rising up to the Creator from the remotest strata of creation, so eager were they to attract this to themselves."[4] What was God to do? He responded by breathing spiritual life into clay and making a new cosmic priest to perform the hierarchical task Lucifer had forsaken in his anarchy. This human being was a spirit that "will embrace matter in the ascensional movement of its own creation, and will establish it once more in the cycle of thanksgiving, of the cosmic Eucharist which has been frustrated by Satan. Thus the World, fallen with its prince, will be liberated from darkness and death by one who was the very child of earth."[5] Unfortunately, Satan therefore turns his attention to this Adam and Eve, the intended cosmic priests. Although Satan is incapable of touching the deep springs of intelligence and freedom, he has more than enough room to maneuver in the realm of sensual delight and material temptation, so he approaches the woman first, and then the man. Bouyer describes the scene:

> Man will yield. The potential Redeemer of the earth will be the supreme conquest of the rebel spirit. Satan, incapable of repressing, will prove himself, alas, only too capable of seduc-

3 Louis Bouyer, *The Meaning of the Monastic Life* (London: Burnes & Oates, 1955), 30.
4 Bouyer, *The Meaning of the Monastic Life*, 30.
5 Bouyer, *The Meaning of the Monastic Life*, 30.

ing that liberty which he had felt surge up beneath him, as a possible taking back by God of the empire which the demon had stolen from him. And that is the second drama, an extension of the first: the fall of man re-echoes the fall of Satan. Instead of the world, in man, being snatched away from the empire of the devil, it was now, through man, thrown into the bondage of sin and death.[6]

With appetites that have been bent (but not broken), perverted (but not destroyed), a world that God pronounced good six times, and very good on an additional seventh time, can be taken in a worldly manner. We have taken the world wrongly, we have mis-taken it, this is our sinful mis-take. Christian doctrine combines a sternly realistic recognition of sin with an amazingly optimistic anthropology. It does not say that our appetites have been so perverted as to desire evil instead of good, it says we confuse a perfect good with an apparent good. In his book *On Evil*, Thomas Aquinas quotes Pseudo-Dionysius when the latter says, "Evil is not the direct object of the will."[7] "No one acts with evil as his goal."[8] "No one makes evil his object when performing an action."[9] And when Thomas uses his own voice to assert the premise, he writes, "The act itself is not willed according as it is disordered, but according to something else, which while the will is seeking it, it incurs the foresaid deordination which it would not will."[10] The paradox remains that we do not choose an act because it is sinful, yet we can choose sinfully. No creature chooses evil, not even the demons, says Thomas ("Sin could not be in demons in the way that they would desire as good for themselves something evil"[11]), but we can be mistaken when we choose and suffer disorder when we desire. We may not have an appetite for poison, but we might mistake poison and eat it.

All mystical authors East or West agree that the person to be cured

---

[6] Bouyer, *The Meaning of the Monastic Life*, 32. I have connected this retelling by Bouyer to man and woman's duty as cosmic priests in "Cosmological Liturgy and a Sensible Priesthood," *New Blackfriars*, vol. 82, no. 960 (February 2001): 76–87.

[7] Thomas Aquinas, *On Evil* (Notre Dame: University of Notre Dame Press, 1995), 135.

[8] Aquinas, *On Evil*, 154.

[9] Aquinas, *On Evil*, 145.

[10] Aquinas, *On Evil*, 30.

[11] Aquinas, *On Evil*, 461.

of sin must begin with purgation. The final unitive stage starts with an initial purgative stage. We must die in order to rise, be stripped in order to be clothed, overcome pride if we are to be overcome by God. We cannot place our eyes upon the Kingdom if we do not take them off ourselves. We cannot love life with God if we do not hate life without him. Without embracing suffering, we cannot be embraced by the Suffering Servant. This purgative way has been described with various images. Here are two from Origen. The first is a reference to Genesis 26:18, where Isaac repairs water wells that had been filled in by the Philistines. Origen writes, "Each one of our souls contains a well of living water. It has in it a buried image of God. It is this well that the hostile powers have blocked up with the earth. But now that our Isaac [Christ] has come, let us welcome his coming and dig out our wells, clearing the earth from them. . . . We shall find living water in them."[12] That each one of our souls contains a well of living water is why Gregory the Great said we may turn inward, as well as upward and forward, but liturgical asceticism must release this flow of living water, and does so only after much digging. Asceticism is positive, since it is for our ultimate refreshment, but the labor expended gives it a negative reputation.

Another image Origen uses is that of cleaning the house for the visit of a King, reminiscent of the woman in Luke 15:8. "It was not outside but *in her house* that the woman who had lost her silver coin found it again. . . . If you light your lamp, and make use of the illumination of the Holy Spirit, you will find the silver coin in you. It could not be seen in you as long as your house was dirty, full of refuse and rubbish, but, rid by the Word of God of that great pile of earth that was weighing you down, let the 'image of the heavenly' shine out in you now."[13] Mystery will come to abide in our hearts, if they are clean, and liturgical asceticism is cleaning the house, preparing the mind, purifying the soul for Mystery's entrance. Mystery always accompanies her bridegroom: she comes from heaven into the visible, hierarchical, sacramental liturgy, and from there she wishes to go more deeply into our hearts by becoming our invisible, personal, mystical liturgy. If we prepare for her arrival.

Asceticism and mysticism share a liturgical unity, and they will

---

[12] Origen, Homily on Genesis 1 and 4, quoted in Olivier Clément, *The Roots of Christian Mysticism* (Hyde Park, NY: New City Press, 1996), 131.

[13] Origen, quoted in Clément, *The Roots of Christian Mysticism*, 131.

not let go of their embrace until the Parousia. Up to that day, we must remain diligent in cleaning the house for Mystery's arrival. The *Sayings of the Desert Fathers* records the following advice from a hermit:

> The devil is like a hostile neighbor and you are like a house. The enemy continually throws all the dirt that he can find into your house. It is your business to throw out whatever he throws in. If you neglect to do this, your house will be so full of mud that you will not be able to get inside. From the moment he begins to throw it in, put it out again, bit by bit: and so with Christ's help your house will remain clean.[14]

The dirt being thrown are the *logismoi* (evil tempting thoughts), and if you neglect to throw them out again, they will pile up into passions and your heart will be so full of mud that Mystery will not be able to get inside. This is the context in which to understand what Eastern Christian asceticism means by the passions. Here "passion" does not mean a strong and vehement feeling for good or ill, instead it means a movement of the soul contrary to nature, a faculty that is no longer upright. Evagrius of Pontus concluded that there are eight logismoi from which may grow the passions, and although we cannot prevent the devil from throwing dirt in, it is up to us to decide whether to throw the temptation back out. Here is the list: "First is that of gluttony, then impurity, avarice, sadness, anger, acedia, vainglory, and last of all, pride. It is not in our power to determine whether we are disturbed by these thoughts, but it is up to us to decide if they are to linger within us or not and whether or not they are to stir up our passions."[15]

Evagrius is following an ancient assessment of the soul that recognizes three faculties in a human being. A person is able to think—this is the *intellective* faculty; a person has appetites that generate desires—this is the *concupiscible* faculty; and a person can be moved to action by having his ire stirred up—this is the *irascible* faculty. In themselves, these faculties are good gifts from God. It is only when

[14] *Sayings of the Desert Fathers*, ch. 11, no. 48, in *The Desert Fathers: Sayings of the Early Christian Monks*, trans. Benedicta Ward (New York: Penguin Books, 2003), 127.
[15] Evagrius, *Praktikos*, in *The Praktikos & Chapters on Prayer* (Kalamazoo: Cistercian Publications, 1981), 6.

they are misused, distorted, and falsified that they become passions. Maximus the Confessor describes a healthy soul by saying, "The soul is moved reasonably when its concupiscible element is qualified by self-mastery, its irascible element cleaves to love and turns away from hate, and the rational element lives with God through prayer and spiritual contemplation."[16] If the intellective faculty is docile to God and yields to his divine Torah, it can handle desire and ire the way a driver can handle the two horses pulling the chariot. But the Fall bent the faculties of the soul: when something went wrong above us (between ourselves and God), something immediately also went wrong within us (between the intellective, concupiscible, and irascible faculties). Disobedience now reigns both inside and out, and Maximus describes an unhealthy soul by saying, "All passionate thoughts either excite the concupiscible, disturb the irascible, or darken the rational element of the soul."[17]

Evagrius has organized the eight logismoi around the three faculties. A distorted *concupiscible* faculty results in gluttony, lust, and avarice; a corrupted *irascible* faculty exhibits itself in sadness, anger, and acedia (a sort of despondent sloth); and when the *intellective* faculty goes wrong, it does so as vainglory and pride. These are the demons on the front line, and people already wounded by them are subsequently attacked by other demons. The ascetical tradition is attentive to the relationship between a principle and its corollary, the vine and its branches, the mother and her daughters. At the moment, I am only interested in looking at the enervating effect of these temptations, so I will neither go beyond these eight nor recite the advice given for battling them, I will only look at the effect they have on our capacity for liturgical mysticism. Let us use Evagrius's brief description of each as our starting point.[18]

(1) *"The thought of gluttony suggests to the monk that he give up his ascetic efforts in short order. It brings to his mind concern over a long illness, scarcity of the commodities of life, and finally lack of care by the physicians."* Evagrius is writing about ascetics in the desert who have taken a vow of literal poverty, but we can apply it easily enough to any

---

[16] Maximus the Confessor, *Four Hundred Chapters on Love*, IV.15 (New York: Paulist Press, 1985), 77.

[17] Maximus, *Four Hundred Chapters on Love*, III.20, p. 63.

[18] The "eight evil thoughts," quoted in the following paragraphs, are defined by Evagrius in *The Praktikos*, in *The Praktikos & Chapters on Prayer*, 16–20.

Christian by recalling John Climacus's definition of poverty as "resignation from care."[19] The ascetic in the desert has made the more dramatic resignation, but the ascetic in the city has more cares to resign from. The thought of gluttony suggests we cannot trust God's providence, and therefore the soul busies itself like an ant in an anthill with preparations to ward off what it fears will be a future calamity. When the mind is focused upon an unnamed fear, it has no capacity for a hopeful future, for a past and fertile memory, or for present and charming delights. Fear distresses, fear worries, fear dreads—and Mystery cannot reside in a milieu of fear. Anxieties allow no room for the hesychasm (silent contemplation) that Mystery intends to import when she comes to dwell in a soul. Like damp wood impedes the spark, fear impedes Mystery's company. Gluttony pushes one's own needs forward egotistically, blocking all else from view. It keeps the soul in disarray, with plots and programs that are too noisy, which keep us from hearing Mystery's still, small voice.

Traces of the *logoi* have been secreted throughout creation by God, but they are overlooked by a gluttonous attitude that treats gifts like utilities. Abraham Heschel suggests that one purpose of the Sabbath law is to disrupt this mindset and bring about healing:

> He who wants to enter the holiness of the day must first lay down the profanity of clattering commerce, of being yoked to toil. He must go away from the screech of dissonant days, from the nervousness and fury of acquisitiveness and the betrayal in embezzling his own life. He must say farewell to manual work and learn to understand that the world has already been created and will survive without the help of man. Six days a week we wrestle with the world, wringing profit from the earth; on the Sabbath we especially care for the seed of eternity planted in the soul. The world has our hands, but our soul belongs to Someone Else. Six days a week we seek to dominate the world, on the seventh day we try to dominate the self.[20]

Dominion over a nervous, gluttonous, and embezzling self is required

---

[19] John Climacus, step 17 of *Ladder of Divine Ascent* (New York: Paulist Press, 1982), 189.

[20] Abraham Heschel, *The Sabbath* (New York: Farrar, Straus & Giroux, 1977), 13.

if Mystery is to take up residence in us. She cannot accompany her bridegroom into a rapacious heart.

(2) *"The demon of impurity impels one to lust after bodies. It attacks more strenuously those who practice continence in the hope that they will give up their practice of this virtue."* We can easily enough connect this remark to the virtue of chastity because chastity defends purity even among those who have not taken a vow of continence. The Catechism quotes *Persona Humana* when it states, "Individuals should be endowed with this virtue according to their state of life [CDF, *Persona humana* 11]" (2349). Chastity is not a weak, timid, puritanical aversion to pleasure; it is a power, a strength, a virtue. According to John Paul II, it "signifies spiritual energy capable of defending love from the perils of selfishness and aggressiveness, and able to advance it towards its full realization."[21] Love is always in need of defense because the demon of impurity ceaselessly stresses selfishness and aggressiveness. Chastity is that defense. Love for another human being is a training drill for loving God, and the demon of lust ruins the opportunity by looking at the person as an object to be exploited. Buber's I–Thou is degraded to an I–It. The personal mystery of the other is overlooked.

A true mystic's chastity is coupled with patience and chivalry; it gives and does not assimilate; it creates space between two persons where secret truths can be brought to bloom; it does not judge by appearance but sees personal beauty (the beauty of the interior person). Mystery can only put down her roots in purity, which is why the Scriptures are adamant that worship be attended by purification. Sin itself can be understood as impurity—not only or even mainly of the sexual kind but an adulteration of mind and will. Mystery will only reside where there is purity because she wants to guide the pure in heart to see God (Matt 5:8). Purity is unmixed, undefiled, and innocent, as are Mary and all the saints.

(3) *"Avarice suggests to the mind a lengthy old age, inability to perform manual labor at some future date, famines that are sure to come, sickness that will visit us, the pinch of poverty, the great shame that comes from accepting the necessities of life from others."* The avaricious person is always eager to procure one more advantage because he can never be sure he has enough, even though the last harvest is already rotting in his overstuffed barns. He does not know that this night his very life

---

[21] John Paul II, Apostolic Exhortation On the Role of the Christian Family in the Modern World *Familiaris Consortio* (November 22, 1981), §33.

may be required of him—and then who will own what he has avariciously accumulated? (Luke 12:20). The avaricious person already shows hints of the upcoming, final vice of pride, because he will feel ashamed not to be independent, self-reliant, sovereign. He does not know that Mystery always requires koinonia and mutuality, which are characteristics of the perichoresis she serves.

The avaricious person thinks that moments of mystery cannot happen unless all conditions are met in advance, and thus he spends so much time arranging favorable conditions that he misses Mystery as she walks by, hand in hand with Christ. The avaricious person thinks he must buttress himself against famine, sickness, poverty before he can be happy, but the demon of avarice has lied to him about this, because Mystery is spiritual and can sovereignly choose the timing of her visit. Her arrival does not depend upon us adequately staffing, training, and arranging our temporal goods. The avaricious man will limit himself to one child so he can afford two cars, not knowing that he need not first own a mansion in the suburbs before Mystery will visit: she comes even to the poorest of Israel who are befriended by God.

(4) *"Sadness tends to come up at times because of the deprivation of one's desires. Certain thoughts first drive the soul to the memory of home and parents, or else to that of one's former life. Now when these thoughts find that the soul offers no resistance but rather follows after them and pours itself out in pleasures that are still only mental in nature, they then seize her and drench her in sadness. On other occasions it accompanies anger."* Mystery's joyfulness is incompatible with a moping disposition. This is not well-placed sadness, appropriate sadness, spiritual sadness; it is brooding caused by a bruised ego, sullenness over the denial of an ill-informed desire, dejection over docility. On occasions, it accompanies anger; on other occasions, anger accompanies it. When the restrictions come from God, we become angry at him; when they come from other persons we become angry at them, even a loved one; and it is a sad spectacle to see someone angry at reality itself when natural restrictions limit the attainment of some fantastic desire. John Climacus compares an angry person to a "voluntary epileptic" and says, "Angry people, because of their self-esteem, make a pitiable site, though they do not realize this themselves. They get angry and then, when thwarted, they become furious."[22] When a person's fan-

---

[22] John Climacus, step 8 of *The Ladder of Divine Ascent*, 149.

tasies create yet stronger desires, the mind is drenched in yet greater sadness upon their disappointment. As a result, thoughts turn away from the asceticism of the moment and retreat to the memory of easier and more pleasant times. The saddened person cannot resonate to Mystery's joyful nature and demeanor. The strings of a harp will not vibrate sympathetically to a tuning fork unless those strings are undamped.

(5) *"The most fierce passion is anger. In fact it is defined as a boiling and stirring up of wrath against one who has given injury—or is thought to have done so. It constantly irritates the soul and above all at the time of prayer it seizes the mind and flashes the picture of the offensive person before one's eyes. If it persists longer it is transformed into indignation."* Mystery is driven away by the two-fisted pummeling of anger and sadness. She must wait for the virtues of peace and fortitude to bring the soul to the calmness that she needs. Turbulent water cannot hold a reflection, and an angry heart cannot hold the image of God. John Cassian says, "No matter what provokes it, anger blinds the soul's eyes, preventing it from seeing the Sun of righteousness."[23] If we are blind, how will we see Mystery in her approach? John Climacus says, "There is no greater obstacle to the presence of the Spirit in us than anger."[24] If anger drives out the Holy Spirit, to whom will Mystery pilot us? An angry spirit is unteachable, so Mystery will not waste her tutelage. Anger may be external, in which case we have forfeited the peace with our neighbor that is required to taste the mystery of the love of God; or it may be internal, in which case we have forfeited the peace with God that is required to taste the mystery of community.

Anger makes a person less likely to listen to reason, and Logos (reason) is the master of Lady Mystery. Anger isolates a person, while on the contrary, Mystery is communal. Indignation refuses to extend pity, while on the contrary, Mystery is concordant ("hearts together"). Indignation asserts rights, while on the contrary, Mystery is humble. John Climacus explains how tenaciously entangled with fallen nature this passion is when he hears Anger say, "I come from many sources and I have more than one father. My mothers are Vainglory, Avarice, Greed. And Lust too. My father is named Conceit. My daughters have the names Remembrance of Wrongs, Hate, Hostility and

---

[23] John Cassian, "On the Eight Vices," in *The Philokalia*, vol. 1 (London: Faber and Faber, 1979), 83.

[24] John Climacus, *The Ladder of Divine Ascent*, 147.

Self-Justification."[25] These are not the kin of Mystery.

(6) *"The demon of acedia—also called the noonday demon—is the one that causes the most serious trouble of all."* Evagrius goes on to describe the noonday demon in an amusing manner. First the demon makes it seem that the sun barely moves and the day is fifty hours long; then he makes the monk look out the window to see if an approaching visitor would provide an excuse to interrupt his work; then he makes the monk calculate how long it is to mealtime; finally, this demon instills a hatred for the place, for the life, and for the labor. It is the reason why the ascetical literature of the desert repeatedly and cease-lessly advises the monk to "stay in his cell," and I think this ascetical advice can be transplanted from the desert to the city as advice for spouses to stay in their marriage, employees to stay honest, the sick to stay hopeful. Do not cease to labor in whatever asceticism your state of life demands of you. *Acedia* means a lethargy or listlessness born from despondency over having to do one's spiritual duties. This is probably how the word came to be translated as "sloth," but it means more than what the Puritans meant by laziness. *Acedia* it is a desire for something less—less strenuous and less toilsome. It will settle for lesser housemates than Mystery. It shares with the devil the expecta-tion that everything good is boring. It is a dissipated soul, scattered and dispersed, one that will not do the labor required to minister to Mystery. The mind flits like a sparrow tied with a string on its foot because the will has not housebroken the moods. Mystery requires a longer fascination than this state of mind wants to give her; the ascent to Mystery requires more exertion than this soul will give her; the charm of Mystery requires more courtesy than this boredom can give her.

(7) *"The spirit of vainglory is most subtle and it readily grows up in the souls of those who practice virtue. It leads them to desire to make their struggles known publicly, to hunt after the praise of men. This in turn leads to their hearing fancied sounds, or crowds of people who touch their clothes. This demon predicts besides that they will attain to the priesthood. It has men knocking at the door, seeking audience with them."* We smile at the picture of such a man, even described from across the centuries, but only so long as we are not looking in a mirror. Vainglory is comical in others, but it stings to have it pointed out in ourselves. It is especially dangerous because it grows greater as we practice the other virtues:

---

[25] John Climacus, *The Ladder of Divine Ascent*, 150–151.

incredibly, this is a vice that feeds on virtues, making it especially dangerous. The man with a vainglorious mind goes back and forth like a shuttlecock between himself and what he thinks others are thinking about him. Therefore he has no peace in his interior conversation, he cannot look on high because he is concerned with the opinion of those around him, and he is more concerned with his current social rank than any happiness that heaven may offer. He would prefer to have other people knocking at his door than to have Mystery knock at his door, because he wonders: *What could she possibly contribute to my glory?*

(8) *"The demon of pride is the cause of the most damaging fall for the soul. For it induces the monk to deny that God is his helper and to consider that he himself is the cause of virtuous actions. Further, he gets a big head in regard to the brethren, considering them stupid because they do not all have this same opinion of him."* Vainglory is similar to pride, but the former wants honor from other human beings, and the latter snatches credit from God. The proud man considers himself the cause of his virtuous actions and salvation, and so denies the most essential feature of the liturgical mysticism offered by God: its gratuitousness. Mystery is free, unforced, supererogatory, and liberating, in contrast to pride that always calculates the value of an action and computes the utility of an effort because it is ultimately seeking self-reliance. Pride is born from *philautia*: self-love. Pride is so full of self-achievement that there is no space for grace. Mystery cannot remain when we have remade the cosmos in our own image, placed ourselves in its center, and taken charge of our own salvation in every detail. The activity of God that puts Mystery in motion is politely declined by the proud man. There will be no Mystery in hell because the proud are so full of themselves that she will not be able to fit. There will be no Mystery in hell because we will not let her turn our *incurvatus in se* right-side out again.

These are the eight logismoi that hinder liturgical mystery. They are the passions (plural) that are the world (singular). Maximus says, "The one who has self-love has all the passions."[26] Isaac the Syrian can see the many in the one, the one in the many. "When we wish to give a collective name to the passions, we call them *world*. And when we wish to designate them specifically according to their names, we call them *passions*."[27] What we are really battling *in toto* is worldliness.

---

[26] Maximus the Confessor, *Four Hundred Chapters on Love*, III.8, p. 62.

[27] Isaac the Syrian, Homily 2, in *The Ascetical Homilies of Saint Isaac the Syrian* (Boston: Holy Transfiguration Monastery, 1984), 14–15.

Christ's bride will not take up residence in a house that is impure. She will not dwell there. Why not? Because the evil thoughts repel Mystery, each in their own way, and altogether. Let the eight logismoi ferment into passions, and self-love reigns, and the world is stripped of Mystery, a condition called "worldliness." Worldliness is caused by haughty cleverness, closed empiricism, profaned secularism, private judgment, desecrated philosophy, coarsened nature, and shortsighted vision, which is why Gregory the Great calls a person wicked for succumbing to worldliness.

> For the wicked, while they neglect in their hearts to go on to the things of eternity, and do not observe that all things present are fleeting, fix their hearts on the love of the present life, and as it were therein construct for themselves the foundation of a long abode, because by desire they are established in earthly things. . . . For one may see great numbers minding temporal things alone, seeking after honors, open-mouthed after the encompassing of good things, looking out for nothing after this life.[28]

This state of affairs has not changed since he described it. The wicked person lives only outwardly, focused only on what is below, and only concerned with the temporary. The good world as God's cosmos has been corrupted into a fallen world of rebellion, and we must know how to battle it if we are to be successful.

An unsuccessful battle plan consists of the frequent but erroneous conclusion that we must abandon the world in order to find Mystery. This is false. Liturgical asceticism does not serve liturgical mysticism by calling upon us to forsake the world but by calling upon us to spiritualize it. Vladimir Solovyov affirms the point by saying, "[T]he purpose of Christian asceticism is not to weaken the flesh, but to strengthen the spirit for the transfiguration of the flesh."[29] Liturgical asceticism does not seek to free the spirit from the body, it seeks to use body and spirit together, freely, for liturgical purpose. Mysticism springs from liturgical asceticism because asceticism quickens the light of Mount Tabor bestowed at liturgy, by which a person sees the world anew,

---

[28] Gregory the Great, *Moralia in Job*, vol. 2 (n.p.: Ex Fontibus, 2012), 224.

[29] Vladimir Solovyov, "The Jews," in *A Solovyov Anthology*, ed. S. L. Frank (London: SCM Press, 1950), 120.

aright, mystically. The world takes on a sacramental hue in this light to reveal its sacrificial potential. In class, Aidan Kavanagh used to define liturgy as "doing the world the way the world was meant to be done," and I shall add that it is seeing the world the way the world was meant to be seen. Without asceticism, God's beautiful world will captivate the passions, arouse gluttony and anger and vainglory; with asceticism, God's beautiful world can arouse doxology and oblation and worship. We do the world either idolatrously or Eucharistically. Liturgical mysticism requires that we resist the temptation to idolize the world.

Asceticism is the fee the Old Adam must pay in order to enjoy communion with God. If it is not paid, then the presence of God will be experienced as hellish, whether now or in eternity. The fee is the mortification of the Old Adam. I include the common, modern definition of "mortify": it is embarrassing, humiliating, it wounds one's pride, it is self-inflicted privation. But mostly I mean it in its etymological sense: the Old Adam is killed dead. We cannot enjoy love of God so long as we trip over our own self-love, and we cannot lift up our hands in *orans* so long as they are weighed down by some temporal good we will not release. Gregory the Great made contrasts between outward and inward, below and above, now and then, and we could say asceticism is the cost of stabilizing each of those pairs. It restores equilibrium to our lives by balancing exterior superficialities with a permanent *interior* truth, balancing earthly preoccupations with the enduring *heights* of beauty, and balancing evanescing goods with a *permanent* and stable goodness. This is not a gnostic movement from corporeal to incorporeal, it is a spiritual adjudication between the impermanent and the abiding, the preparatory and the final, the pathway and the home. We only know how to do the world, liturgically, when the world does not control us, but we master the world. And if I need to say it one more time, this is not a battle with material things, it is a battle with Satan who conducts warfare against us with those material things. Asceticism sensitizes us more profoundly to truth, beauty, and goodness by putting us in contact with God, their source. Asceticism purifies our prayer. Abba Isaiah of Scetis warns against asking God for forgiveness when we hold a grudge against our fellow human being, because "[s]uch a person does not pray with the intellect, but ignorantly with the lips, for one who truly desires to pray with the intellect to God, in the Holy Spirit, and with a pure heart, searches his heart before praying. . . . Unless you have managed to do these things, then you are praying in vain."[30] Do asceticism before prayer, or prayer is in vain. Liturgical asceticism makes *logike latreia* possible, and then liturgical mysticism can find pasture in us.

The sacraments cannot take root in hardened hearts, like seeds cannot take root on the soil of a beaten path. The sinful eye registers no sight not egotistical, therefore it cannot see the mysteries of the Savior in the mirror of the sacraments. Asceticism is necessary if liturgical theology is going to break the dynamics of self-love and a sacrament can reach its end. In order for the sacraments to accomplish their purpose in us, we must go to the cross. The sacraments of initiation lay the cross over the abyss from sin to sanctity so we may traverse it; the sacraments at the service of communion are trained by the self-renunciation the cross effects; and the sacraments of healing depend upon a power that floods us from the cross. And the chief of the sacraments, the Eucharist, is served, according to Catherine of Siena, on the table of the cross. She records the divine dictation of God saying to her, "Such souls glory in the shame of my only-begotten Son. . . . [And] so these also run to the table of the most holy cross, in love with my love and hungry for the food of souls. They want to be of service to their neighbors in pain and suffering, and to learn and preserve the virtues well bearing the marks of Christ in their bodies."[31] We meet the glorified Christ at the Eucharistic table, and our guide must be the apostle Thomas who shows us where to place our fingers and hand. Charles Journet says that Christ is made present in transubstantiation according to the state in which Christ is now, which is his glorious state, already entered into. But although that is his state, it is not what he communicates to us in the sacrament.

> He will come in His glorious state; however, certainly not in order to touch us by His glory, but in order to "proclaim his death," to actualize according to our intention the unique act of redemption. He will come with His redemptive act. Between His glory and our sin he will interpose His bloody Cross. . . . We know that there is but a blanket of sacramental appearances which separate us from Paradise . . . [but] he

---

[30] Abba Isaiah of Scetis, *Ascetic Discourses* (Kalamazoo, MI: Cistercian Press, 2002), 139–140.
[31] Catherine of Siena, *The Dialogue*, The Classics of Western Spirituality (New York: Paulist Press, 1980), 144.

interposes his Cross tween himself and us, and the more he presses us close to his heart, the more deeply the cross penetrates into our flesh to crucify us.[32]

Liturgical asceticism is feeling the penetration of the cross into our ego.

This mysticism is liturgical because it operates within a realm that Pavel Florensky calls *ecclesiality*, which he describes as being "how human beings experience truth in its liturgical, mystical, and dogmatic dimensions. It is the new life in the Spirit; it is the beauty of new life in Absolute Beauty, understood as order and wholeness, and it is one with Truth and Goodness."[33] Ecclesiality is where fragmentation is healed and contradiction resolves as antinomy. Antinomy is crucial for sane theology because antinomy is aware that "life is infinitely fuller than rational definitions and therefore no formula can encompass all the fullness of life."[34] This accounts for the apophatic quality of mystical theology. Florensky admits that the knowable world is cracked and that reason is fragmented, but rather than pretending this is not the case we should rather commit ourselves to healing them both. How? It turns out that the epistemological problem must have a religious solution. "Only the purified God-bearing mind of saintly ascetics is *somewhat* more whole. In this mind, the healing of the fissures and cracks has begun; the sickness of being is being cured; the wounds of the world are being healed."[35] The God-bearing mind of the saint, which sees the world by the light of Mount Tabor, is the mind of a liturgical theologian. It is a body and soul under the illumination of the Holy Spirit, a lived state of liturgical prayer, all flame. It is the activity of a theologian soul who has been made one with Christ, the true Theologian.

The mystical darkness is inscribed on our life by Mystery, which it is liturgy's business to celebrate. Discipleship in Christ (liturgical asceticism) sacramentalizes us because liturgy draws us into the hypostatic union that existed in him personally. G. L. Prestige discusses the origin of the Greek word *hypostasis*, saying that the ancient world

[32] Charles Journet, *The Mass: The Presence of the Sacrifice of the Cross* (South Bend, IN: Saint Augustine's Press, 2008), 64, 66.
[33] Richard Gustafson, introduction to Pavel Florensky, *The Pillar and Ground of the Truth* (Princeton: Princeton University Press, 1997), xiv.
[34] Florensky, *The Pillar and Ground of the Truth*, 108.
[35] Florensky, *The Pillar and Ground of the Truth*, 118.

used it to name the dregs of wine in a cask. Thus hypostasis came to denote the hidden part of any object down below, the underlying state or reality of a thing, and so was translated into Latin as the *sub-stance* of a thing. It occurs in Hebrews 11:1: "Faith is the [hypostasis] of things hoped for." Benedict XVI points out in *Spe Salvi* that Thomas Aquinas understood this verse by using the terminology of the philosophical tradition of the time. Faith, said Thomas, is a *habitus* (i.e., "a stable disposition of the spirit, through which eternal life takes root in us and reason is led to consent to what it does not see"[36]). Benedict XVI concludes that faith as an embryo means there is already present in us the things that are hoped for, and this creates certainty. In other words, the verse does not mean a subjective reaching out toward an absent good, rather it says that faith gives us something objectively real. So the Pope emeritus concludes, "[F]aith draws the future into the present, so that it is no longer simply a 'not yet.' The fact that this future exists changes the present; the present is touched by the future reality."[37]

Referring again to Gregory the Great's three categories of inward, above, and what is to come, we may say that faith is the *inward* hypostasis of things hoped for, that come from *above,* and surpass our current "not yet" by drawing the *future* into the present. To my ears, this is a fine definition of liturgical mysticism: the Paschal mystery hypostasizing in our hearts. Liturgy's business is to celebrate the Paschal mystery, and when it does, the mystery hypostasizes in us, descends to us, takes up its home in us, becomes the substance of our lives. The hypostasis of Christ culminated in the Paschal mystery, which now flows, crystal clear, as the water of life, from the throne of God and of the Lamb (Rev 22:1) and pools up in two places. First, it is celebrated visibly in the sacramental liturgy, and second, it settles hypostatically into the invisible liturgy of our heart. The two liturgies are connected, which is why our mystical life depends upon repetitive return to the altar of the Lord every eighth day. Liturgical asceticism must perform an alteration on the heart so our hearts will fit the liturgical mysticism God is tailoring for it. Christ's God-manhood is the prototype of the icon we are mystically becoming. When it mystically hypostasizes in our substance, then Christ's Church, his mystery, will

---

[36] Benedict XVI, Encyclical Letter on Christian Hope *Spe Salvi* (November 30, 2007), §7.

[37] Benedict XVI, *Spe Salvi*, §7.

be beautiful in us, as Ambrose said about his newly baptized catechumens: "The Church is beautiful in them."[38] He reverses our ordinary grammar by not speaking about the church we go into, but about the Church that comes into us. Christ wants to make us perfect liturgists, like himself, glorifying the Father; therefore he disciplines us with the rod of asceticism and gifts us with the balm of Mystery.

Christ is truth, beauty, and goodness in union. On the one hand, the Greek tradition saw a connection between the second and third of the three terms in their word *kallos*. *Philokalia* means "love of beauty/goodness" (which is why it was used as a title for a five volume collection of writings on asceticism). *Kallos* means beautiful to look at, good, excellent in nature, praiseworthy, honorable, virtuous. On the other hand, Plato saw a connection between the first and second of the three terms when he said that beauty is the splendor of truth, from *splendere*, "to shine." When truth shines, there is beauty. This truth will be most fully splendored when it is manifested at the highest created level, which is personhood, so Paul Evdokimov adds that the splendor of truth "does not exist in the abstract. In its fullness, truth requires a personalization and seeks to be enhypostazied [*sic*], that is, rooted and grounded in a person."[39] Christ is the personalization of eternal truth in his human hypostasis and is the most splendid truth we know (*splendidus*, bright, shining, glittering, sumptuous, gorgeous, grand, distinguished, noble). Living in this light shining from the Lord in his liturgy would be living in liturgical mysticism. Liturgy is mystical, mystery is liturgical.

---

[38] Ambrose, *On the Mysteries* 7.39, in *Nicene and Post-Nicene Fathers*, vol. 10, Second Series, *Ambrose: Select Works and Letters*, ed. Philip Schaff (Peabody, Massachusetts: Hendrickson, 1996), 322.

[39] Paul Evdokimov, *The Art of the Icon: A Theology of Beauty* (Redondo Beach, CA: Oakwood, 1990), 24.

CHAPTER 5

THE PATH THROUGH CROSS
TO RESURRECTION

"FOR WE ARE NOT CONTENDING against flesh and blood, but against the principalities, against the powers, against the world rulers of this present darkness, against the spiritual hosts of wickedness in the heavenly places" (Eph 6:12). Liturgical mysticism is the life of the resurrection taking hold in us, but it acknowledges that our path to heaven goes through the valley of the shadow of death, our jubilant life comes only after a sickness unto death has been healed, the resurrected life follows the crucified life. This is so because there are powers or principalities or rulers that hold this world captive, from which we will never escape without a personal share in Christ's victory, which is our personal liturgy, the liturgy in our person. Satan's insurrection broke the celestial hierarchy, and the human Fall followed quickly after, so now we live without hierarchy, in anarchy. No, worse: we live under a different *arche*. The world is captive to spiritual powers of rebellion, disobedience, blindness. So when Christ entered this world, it killed him. In so doing, it killed itself, as Schmemann explains:

> The body of Christ is not and can never be of this world. "This world" condemned Christ, the bearer of new life, to death and by doing this it has condemned itself to death. The new life, which shone forth from the grave, is the life of the "new eon," of the age, which in terms of this world is still "to come." The

descent of the Holy Spirit at Pentecost, by inaugurating a new eon, announced the end of this world, for as no one can partake of the "new life" without dying in the baptismal death, no one can have Christ as his life unless he has died and is constantly dying to this world: "for ye are dead and your life is hid with Christ in God" (Col. 3:3). But then nothing which is of this world—no institution, no society, no church—can be identified with the new eon, the new being. The most perfect Christian community—be it completely separated from the evils of the world—as a community is still of this world, living its life, depending on it. It is only by passing into the new eon, by an anticipation—in faith, hope and love—of the world to come, that a community can partake of the Body of Christ, and indeed manifest itself as the Body of Christ. The Body of Christ can never be "part" of this world, for Christ has ascended into heaven and his Kingdom is Heaven.[1]

To redeem this world, the powers and principalities must be defeated and replaced with a restored *arche*, a *hierus-arche*, a priestly power that unites us to the Son of Man, which is how "hierarchy" should be understood according to Louis Bouyer.

The hierarchy, understood as it should be, is only the communication network through the body, which, by appropriate organs, binds it to its Head, the historical Christ, who died and rose in the heart of history and offers life that belongs to all its people. This life, though not properly theirs by the nature of things, is their life in the Spirit of Christ, of God, in truth and love, which are inseparable.[2]

God has designed a place of pilgrimage in the flesh of Christ, at which the latreutic cycle of agape and eucharistia can be rebooted, and because Christ took flesh he is able to unite us to himself. There are now two worlds, one dying and one life-giving, and they are contrasted in every way: by their heads (Satan or Christ), by their activity (diabol-

---

[1] Schmemann, "Theology and Eucharist," in *Liturgy and Tradition*, ed. Thomas Fisch (Crestwood, NY: St. Vladimir's Seminary Press, 1990), 78.
[2] Louis Bouyer, *The Church Of God: Body of Christ and Temple of the Spirit* (San Francisco: Ignatius Press, 2011), 456.

ical or symbolical), by their posture (independent or obedient), and by their principles (rebellion or filiality). The transfer process from the former to the latter world constitutes the conversion therapy of the catechumenate, with its regular exorcisms. An exorcism restores something to its proper owner, and those who will be recapitulated in Christ, who is head of the body (Col 1:18), must be refitted with their new mind by undergoing the cross and resurrection themselves. The historical truth must become, for them, a mystical truth.

I am therefore not being flippant, then, when I take up a phrase that normally lives in the land of liturgy and apply it to the crucifixion. We speak of "full, active, and conscious participation" in liturgy, which usually conjures up disputes over hymn selection and extraordinary ministers of communion, but I would like to instead apply that liturgical platitude to Christ's death and consider full, active, and conscious participation in the cross. This serves to remind us that any reform of the liturgy does not have the aim of bringing us closer to the rubrical style of some given historical era, it has the purpose of bringing us closer to Christ. The tip of the liturgical iceberg is the public ceremony, but it is attached to a massive reality below the waterline, and in order to fully comprehend liturgy, we must appreciate the saving economy that it epiphanizes, and that reaches all the way back to a decision made by the Trinity. Virgil Michel expresses this in his description of liturgy's origin:

> The liturgy, through Christ, comes from the Father, the eternal source of the divine life in the Trinity. It in turn addresses itself in a special way to the Father, rendering him the homage and the glory of which it is capable through the power of Christ. The flow of divine life between the eternal Father and the Church is achieved and completed through the operation of the Holy Ghost.
>
> The liturgy, reaching from God to man, and connecting man to the fullness of the Godhead, is the action of the Trinity in the Church. The Church in her liturgy partakes of the life of the divine society of the three persons in God.[3]

The perichoresis of that Trinity was kenotically extended to invite our

---

[3] Virgil Michel, O.S.B., *The Liturgy of the Church, according to the Roman Rite* (New York: Macmillan, 1937), 40.

ascent into eternal life, but we must synergistically join Jesus at the center point of that timeline, which is the cross, stretching between the protological alpha and the eschatological omega. Everything leads up to it, and everything flows out of it. And when Mother Church said at the Second Vatican Council that she "earnestly desires that all the faithful should be led to that fully conscious, and active participation in liturgical celebrations which is demanded by the very nature of the liturgy," and which is the "right and duty [of Christian people] by reason of their baptism,"[4] she was not speaking about their right to rites. She was speaking about their right to life. This kind of participation, she went on to say in the same paragraph, confirms the Christian's identity in a chosen race, a royal priesthood, a holy nation, and a redeemed people. The reason to restore and promote the sacred liturgy is so that the faithful may derive from it the true Christian spirit. And just what is the true Christian spirit that we are to derive from the liturgy? The one found in Christ, the one which is found in Christ's hypostatic union.

In Jesus, a human will was finally fully conformed to the will of God—something intended for the first Adam, but not accomplished. Jesus emptied himself into only one desire: to obey and love and be near the Father. George MacDonald puts it this way:

> [Jesus's] whole thought, his whole delight, was in the thought, in the will, in the being of his Father. The joy of the Lord's life, that which made it life to him, was the Father; of him he was always thinking, to him he was always turning. I suppose most men have some thought of pleasure or satisfaction or strength to which they turn when action pauses, life becomes for a moment still, and the wheel sleeps on its own swiftness: with Jesus it needed no pause of action, no rush of renewed consciousness, to send him home; his thought was ever and always his Father. To its home in the heart of the Father his heart ever turned. That was his treasure-house, the jewel of his mind, the mystery of his gladness, claiming all degrees and shades of delight, from peace and calmest content to ecstasy. His life was hid in God.[5]

---

4   Pope Paul VI, Constitution on the Sacred Liturgy *Sacrosanctum Concilium* (December 4, 1963), §14.

5   George MacDonald, *Unspoken Sermons, First, Second and Third Series* (Whitehorn, CA: Johannsen, 1999), 171.

This attitude was present throughout the life of Jesus, as we are privileged to glimpse in the Gospels. Jesus's one will was to do the will of the one who sent him. Whatever he had came from his Father in heaven. "Why do you call me good? No one is good but God alone" (Mark 10:18; Luke 18:19). And when the hour came when each of his disciples scattered, an hour we remember with shame because we know we would have done the same, he says he will not be alone "for the Father is with me" (John 16:32).

Insofar as the cross was required for our redemption, it was the Father's will for his Son, and insofar as it was his Father's will, Jesus willingly embraced it. In Christian typological reading of the Old Testament, the most frequently mentioned type of Christ was Moses, of course. Moses was prophet, priest, and king all rolled into one. But the second most frequently mentioned type of Jesus was Isaac for willingly submitting to Abraham's raised knife. Rabbinic interpretation had already marveled at Isaac's obedience when it calculated the age of an old and frail father intending to sacrifice a young and strong son. Did a sacrifice happen in Genesis 22? If we think sacrifice means death, we might be distracted to the ram in the thicket. But if we remember that sacrifice means willing obedience, then we are led to realize that it was no less Abraham's sacrifice than it was Isaac's, which presents a parallel for Calvary. Whose sacrifice is it on Calvary? No less God the Father's than God the Son's. And if we follow Christ down the mystical path toward complete union with the Father, we will have to pause with him here. We are happy enough to embrace the prophet on the shores of Galilee, the teacher of love, the miracle worker and parable spinner, but we cannot speed past this fact: if we are to fully, consciously, and actively participate in the life of Christ, then we must embrace what he embraced. He embraced the cross, from love, out of obedience.

Paul Claudel's reflections on the crucifixion are gathered in a meditation on the Apostle's Creed titled *I Believe in God*. When Jesus was trying to get across to his disciples what their discipleship would involve, particularly the mother of the sons of Zebedee, he talked about servants and slaves and declared, "[T]he Son of man came not to be served but to serve, and to give his life as a ransom for many" (Matt 20:28). Claudel observes, centuries later, "Well, if it is true that you came to serve, I daresay you got what you were after!" and then criticizes the casual attitude we have toward Christ in the liturgy: "It is painful to know that you are here at our disposal and that we can think of no better use for you than to help pass that tedious half hour before dinner on Sunday."[6] Familiarity has deadened our amazement. "A god is about to die before our eyes. . . . On the very brink of this act by which all things exist he found no way to defend himself from the shaft of love. The earth trembles and gapes, the curtain of the temple is torn from top to bottom, the graves vomit up their dead. There is a universal shuddering of the whole creation around the cross. On all sides things break asunder and yawn open."[7] The first creation, the one we stained with sin, had to be split open so that the seed of new life could find its way to the surface. And to plant such a seed in ourselves, we, too, must be split open. The blows of the hammer upon the nails in his hands must be redirected to us in order to crack us open. But this feels impossible, Claudel laments. "I feel that I have undertaken something beyond my strength. These wings of wood, how can I adjust them to sit on my shoulders?"[8]

Francis Libermann spoke frequently about God placing us on a cross. "I see that you are firmly nailed to the cross and that your heart is pierced by a thousand swords of sorrow."[9] Use them, he advises, to advance God's work to the sanctification of your soul. "My dear child: it seems that the good Lord wants you on the Cross and I am glad that it is so."[10] "Do not set limits to the crosses you are willing to bear. Accept all that come as so many precious stones and be afraid to let any escape from your grasp."[11] Each cross gives the opportunity to practice self-renunciation, which, he says, is why God has placed us here. "Crosses, as it were, take us out of ourselves more and more, they empty us of ourselves and fill us with God; they make us receptive and docile to the impressions and impulses of divine grace; they make us humble and small in our own eyes and distrustful of self; they make us live in entire dependence on Jesus, our only love, and realizing that dependence, we are aware of our poverty, weakness,

6 Paul Claudel, *I Believe in God: A Meditation on the Apostles' Creed*, ed. Agnes du Sarment (New York: Holt, Rinehart and Winston, 1963), 109.
7 Claudel, *I Believe in God*, 115.
8 Claudel, *I Believe in God*, 124.
9 Francis Libermann, *The Spiritual Letters of the Venerable Francis Libermann*, vol. 1, "Letters to Religious Sisters and Aspirants," in Duquesne Studies, Spiritan Series 5, ed. Walter Van De Putte (Pittsburgh: Duquesne University Press, 1964), 99.
10 Libermann, *The Spiritual Letters*, 1:152.
11 Libermann, *The Spiritual Letters*, 1:144.

and wretchedness."[12] Carry only the particular cross which Divine Goodness sends each day, but carry it as long as God leaves it with you, because when "He plants His Cross in your soul and immolates you to His divine love,"[13] then you will progress into holiness. "Do you understand now how the Cross produces these delightful fruits in you?"[14] "You cannot be sanctified without crosses . . . [and] Jesus could not rise and ascend into heaven, until He had died upon the cross."[15] "The best moments of your life . . . are those spent upon the cross" because "it is here that Jesus is always to be found."[16]

Jesus did not need to die, for he was born without the original curse and was never out of communion with the source of life, his Father. He died nevertheless in order to crack open the door through which we may enter into eternal life. Bouyer is blunt about the matter: "Christ died for us, not in order to dispense us from dying, but rather to make us capable of dying efficaciously."[17] Our dying must be full, we must actively embrace it, and we must do so consciously.

> Rightly understood [Bouyer continues], the imitation of Christ is the very essence of the Christian life. We must have in us the mind that Christ had; we must be crucified and buried and rise with him. This, of course, does not mean that we fallen human beings are to copy clumsily the God-man. The whole matter is a mystery signifying that we are to be grafted upon him so that the same life which was in him and which he has come to give us may develop in us as in him and produce in us the same fruits of sanctity and love that it produced in him.[18]

Liturgical mysticism consists of being grafted upon Christ so that

---

12 Libermann, *The Spiritual Letters*, 1:9.

13 Francis Libermann, *The Spiritual Letters of the Venerable Francis Libermann*, vol. 2, "Letters to People in the World," in Duquesne Studies, Spiritan Series 6, ed. Walter Van De Putte (Pittsburgh: Duquesne University Press, 1964), 304.

14 Libermann, *The Spiritual Letters*, 2:305.

15 Francis Libermann, *The Spiritual Letters of the Venerable Francis Libermann*, vol. 4, "Letters to Clergy and Religious," in Duquesne Studies, Spiritan Series 8, ed. Walter Van De Putte (Pittsburgh: Duquesne University Press, 1964), 309.

16 Libermann, *The Spiritual Letters*, 4:354.

17 Louis Bouyer, *The Paschal Mystery: Meditations on the Last Three Days of Holy Week* (Chicago: Henry Regnery, 1950), xiv.

18 Bouyer, *The Paschal Mystery*, xv.

his life may develop in us and produce the fruits it produced in him. Astonishing! Jesus is the Lord, *Adonai,* the *Kyrios,* the corporeal dwelling place of divinity—and yet human beings in the likeness of the terrestrial Adam are "now called to resemble the heavenly Adam. Baptized in him, they would 'put him on.'"[19]

We dig our toe in the sand in humility, either false or real, and confess that we do not think we can resemble Christ. We are content to downgrade the mystical faith to a religious morality, hoping to keep just enough of the Ten Commandments to squeeze past judgment day. But the divine economy does not plan on stopping short. The Holy Spirit will not stop his disciplines (asceticism) until we are perfect (mystics), as our Father in heaven is perfect. That is the closing promise of those marching orders to evangelical perfection called the Beatitudes. In their spirit, Blessed Columba Marmion asks, "What in fact is a Christian? 'Another Christ,' all antiquity replies."[20] And what is the life the Christian lives? "A list of observances? In nowise. It is the life of Christ within us, and all that Christ has appointed to maintain this life in us; it is the Divine life overflowing from the bosom of the Father into Christ Jesus and, through Him, into our soul."[21] "God not only wills that we should be saved, but that we should become saints."[22] "God is not content and never will be content . . . with a natural morality or religion; He wills us to act as children of a divine race."[23]

The liturgical mysteries, then, are not only events in the biography of the Nazarene, buried under the dust of time, taken out to ogle on days of obligation. In the Triduum we do not only look at the past but at *our future* and what it will cost in the present moment of our lives. Our participation in the Paschal mystery is full, conscious, and active because, Marmion says, Christ attaches a grace to each of his mysteries "to help us to reproduce within ourselves His divine

[19] Bouyer, *The Paschal Mystery,* xv.
[20] Columba Marmion, *Christ: The Ideal of the Monk* (London & Edinburgh: Sands; and St. Louis: Herder, 1922), 124.
[21] Marmion, *Christ: The Ideal of the Monk,* 137.
[22] Columba Marmion, *Christ in His Mysteries* (London & Edinburgh: Sands; and St. Louis: B. Herder, 1931), 386–387.
[23] Columba Marmion, *Life of the Soul* (Bethesda, MD: Zaccheus Press, 2005), 61. Also, "As St. Thomas says, this grace is a participated similitude of the divine nature: *Participata similitudo divinae naturae.* To employ a theological word, grace is deiform because it places in us a divine similitude." *Christ in His Mysteries,* 48.

features in order to make us like unto Him."[24] No Nestorianism in Christology, no Nestorianism in soteriology: we are to become more than images of the human half of Jesus, we are to become images of the whole Christ, the hypostatic union who is God and man. God plans a *theandric* existence for us. We are to become a *sequela Christi*, Benedict XVI says.

> Sequela of Christ does not mean: imitating the man Jesus. This type of attempt would necessarily fail—it would be an anachronism. The Sequela of Christ has a much higher goal: to be assimilated into Christ, that is to attain union with God. . . . Man is not satisfied with solutions beneath the level of divinization. But all the roads offered by the "serpent" (Genesis 3:5), that is to say, by mundane knowledge, fail. The only path is communion with Christ, achieved in sacramental life. The Sequela of Christ is not a question of morality, but a "mysteric" theme—an ensemble of divine action and our response. . . . The Sequela of Christ is participation in the cross, uniting oneself to his love, to the transformation of our life, which becomes the birth of the new man, created according to God (see Ephesians 4:24). Whoever omits the cross, omits the essence of Christianity (see 1 Corinthians 2:2).[25]

The synergistic ascent into deification is a mysteric ensemble.

This death is hard for creatures like ourselves, so we must practice it. Constantly. We must train (askesis) for it by dying daily. Liturgical asceticism is being made more Christoform, which is liturgical mysticism being birthed. It is how the mystery celebrated liturgically becomes the mystery loved and lived. It is the union of sacramental liturgy and personal liturgy. The mystery of the hierarchical liturgy clings to us as we leave the Church, like the scent of incense clinging to our clothes, that we may practice the Paschal mystery fully and consciously and actively in places of the heart that only God sees, mystical places. For the place where we confront our Old Adam in order to put him to death is within the depths of our hearts. In our

---

[24] Marmion, *Christ in His Mysteries*, 233.

[25] Joseph Cardinal Ratzinger, Address to Catechists and Religion Teachers (December 12, 2000), II.3, https://zenit.org/articles/cardinal-ratzinger-on-the-new-evangelization/.

hearts the struggle between the vices and virtues goes on, and it takes a sharp sword to make the fine cut that will remove the passions from our heart without stopping its beating. Such a sword God wields. Claudel says, "God came to pierce each soul; it was His way of opening a passage for Himself."

> External circumstances, the practical life in which we are engaged, only allow us to live on the crust, to use the most superficial part, not necessarily the worst but the least authentic part of ourselves. Only profound emotion, the weight and painful pressure of harsh and turbulent events, reach down to the gushing salutary vein in the depths of us. Someone has fought his way through to us. Someone is urging us to say outright the real name, our own real name.[26]

With all this talk about piercing and pressuring and crucifying, what would cause us to actively pursue it? It is a deep mystery, and at this depth, faith works by its own logic, frequently turning our expectations upside down. Claudel says we rush to the general resurrection from our grave because we desire judgment. A strange thought. Often enough, in our present life, we skulk along the rear wall to avoid the gaze of God, but Claudel says that deep down we desire it: "Our conscience has found what it longed for above all else: a Judge. . . . There are so many things heaped up inside us all ready and only waiting to become an answer for the question to be put. A question, a challenge, a presence."[27] "On the day of the Last Judgment, it is not only the Judge who will descend from heaven, the whole world will rush forth to meet him."[28]

George MacDonald picks up a passage from the Book of Revelations to explain this paradox. The seventeenth verse of chapter two in the Book of Revelation says, "To him who conquers I will give some of the hidden manna, and I will give him a white stone, with a new name written on the stone which no one knows except him who receives it." What name is the Apocalypse talking about? Not one of the ordinary names we go by now. "A name of the ordinary kind in this world, has nothing essential in it. It is but a label by which one

---

[26] Claudel, *I Believe in God*, 163.
[27] Claudel, *Lord, Teach Us to Pray* (London: Dennis Dobson, 1942), 19.
[28] Claudel, *I Believe in God*, 151.

man and a scrap of his external history may be known from another man and a scrap of his history."[29] We have these kinds of names in abundance—from our tribe and our employer and the state. But Mac-Donald says deep down we want our true name. "The true name is one which expresses the character, the nature, the being, the *meaning* of the person who hears it. It is the man's own symbol—his soul's picture, in a word—the sign which belongs to him and to no one else."[30] How do we get such a name? The answer is obvious. In fact, we know the answer, unconsciously, and conversion is the process of being fully conscious of the answer. Conversion means coming to an active desire for the judgment whereupon we will receive our name.

MacDonald asks three questions about it: (1) Who can give a man this, his own name? God alone. For no one but God sees what the man is, or even, seeing what he is, could express in a *name-word* the sum and harmony of what he sees. (2) To whom is this name given? To him that overcomes. (3) When is it given? When he has overcome. And thus the ensemble of grace and free will enters the stage.

> Does God then not know what a man is going to become? As surely as he sees the oak which he put there lying in the heart of the acorn. Why then does he wait till the man has become by overcoming ere he settles what his name shall be? He does not wait; he knows his name from the first. But as—although repentance comes because God pardons—yet the man becomes aware of the pardon only in the repentance; so it is only when the man has become his name that God gives him the stone with the name upon it. . . .
>
> God foresees that from the first, because he made it so; but the tree of the soul, before its blossom comes, cannot understand what blossom it is to bear, and could not know what the word meant. . . . Such a name cannot be given until the man *is* the name. To tell the name is to seal the success—to say "In thee I am well pleased."[31]

We must kiss the cross on the way to receiving our white stone, desir-

---

[29] George MacDonald, *Unspoken Sermons,* Series I, II, III in one volume (White-horn, CA: Johannsen, 1999), 70–71.

[30] MacDonald, *Unspoken Sermons,* 71.

[31] MacDonald, *Unspoken Sermons,* 71–72.

ing that judgment, that purgation, that purification fully, consciously, and actively. Such a desire is what it means to believe in the resurrection.

We believe in all kinds of facts and truths, but surely different kinds of facts and truths call for different kinds of belief, and furthermore, the proper kind of belief should be called forth from the thing believed and not merely the subject believing. This was the lesson learned from Holmer in chapter one when he insisted that the object, not the subject, determines our latria and summons forth a commitment from us appropriate to the occasion. Some kinds of knowledge can be checked out of the library, but there is another kind of knowledge—wisdom, I would say—which must be received personally, mystically, by each new person. Such truths require something of the believing subject. Something different is required of me to believe the weatherman when he tells me tomorrow will be sunny, than is required of me to believe my wife when she tells me she loves me. Different degrees of commitment by the believing subject are required for different kinds of facts, and the different degree of commitment is created by the object of knowledge.

This is what I have in mind when I ask: *What would it mean to believe in the resurrection? What kind of person must someone become in order to believe in the resurrection?* This means neither belief in the past historical fact that Jesus was raised nor belief in one's future, continued existence. It means believing in the resurrection as a present and influential fact in one's own life. What would be required for the resurrection to operate in one's daily liturgical mysticism? I will suggest three names for the subjective condition required to believe this objective truth, and though I am naming it with a triplet, I am only describing one state.

First, mystical belief in the resurrection may be called *faith*. This means both the beginning touch of faith (repentance), and its greater extension into our lives (conversion), and its daily saturation of our mind (liturgical mysticism). Faith operates in a "new mind" (a *meta nous*), for which a modification of the human being is needed. We do receive new minds from time to time, and with a little effort you can think of some ordinary examples. There was that book that opened up a whole new way of seeing things; or that teacher who made the penny drop; or an old activity might take on an entirely new meaning upon falling in love because teleology conditions meaning. But in the case we are discussing here, concerning the resurrection, the creation of a new mind capable of faith must involve synergy with the Holy Spirit. No one can say "Jesus is Lord" except by the Holy Spirit (1 Cor 12:3). Do we really want the resurrection? Lively faith will make us dissatisfied with what is merely to our advantage now, below, and outside, in the terms of Gregory the Great again, and conversion awakens us to this greater dimension by glory, honor, exaltation, splendor, and especially by the combination of beauty and goodness the Greeks called *kallos*.

We have been told that this material world is all there is, that our present life is all there is, but Christianity believes that this world has a sacramental scent and every person is beckoned to eternity. We should be able to smell this in the sacramental celebrations of liturgical mystery. What if we really did believe that a human being is made for resurrection and eternal life? Would we not treat the human being differently, whether at the end of life or in the womb? A human being's whole existence would progress on the crest of a wave from potentiality to actuality, and to really believe there is something everlasting after the temporal would change how we behave during this interim. A day's occasion would look different if we measured it against the horizon of eternity than if we measured it against the horizon of four score years of earthly life. Hugo Rahner says we would behave differently if we stood at the exact midpoint between heaven and earth.

> Only such a man can accept and lovingly embrace the world—which includes himself—as God's handiwork, and, at the same time, toss it aside as a child would toss a toy of which it had wearied, in order then to soar upward into the 'blessed seriousness' which is God alone. [32]
>
> He who plays after this fashion is the "grave-merry" man ... he is a man with an easy gaiety of spirit, one might almost say a man of spiritual elegance, a man who feels himself to be living in invincible security; but he is also a man of tragedy, a man of laughter and tears, a man, indeed, of gentle irony, for he sees through the tragically ridiculous masks of the game of life and has taken the measure of the cramping boundaries of our earthly existence. [33]

---

[32] Hugo Rahner, *Man at Play* (New York: Herder and Herder, 1972), 39.
[33] Hugo Rahner, *Man at Play*, 27.

This is a description of an elegant person of faith for whom *everything* would be different: his experience of time and history and matter would be different; he would desire differently and perhaps different things; he would conduct his work, his play, his vocation differently. That's a first explanation of what it would mean to believe in the resurrection. Such a person would see with a mystical mind that sees the world, and his own life, as they ought to be seen.

Second, mystical belief in the resurrection may be called *love*. An explanation of this comes from a surprising source—the philosopher Ludwig Wittgenstein. Born into a Jewish family, and living in relative agnosticism for part of his life, he thought his way into religious questions, and in *Culture and Value* he connects faith with love:

> What inclines even me to believe in Christ's Resurrection? It is as though I play with the thought.—If he did not rise from the dead, then he decomposed in the grave like any other man. He is dead and decomposed. In that case he is a teacher like any other and can no longer help; and once more we are orphaned and alone. So we have to content ourselves with wisdom and speculation. . . .
>
> But if I am to be *really* saved,—what I need is certainty—not wisdom, dreams or speculation—and this certainty is faith. And faith is faith in what is needed by my heart, my soul, not my speculative intelligence. . . .
>
> Perhaps we can say: Only love can believe the Resurrection. Or: It is love that believes the Resurrection.[34]

Faith and love co-inhere. Faith aligns our hearts with God's heart, and his heart is full of love, so the mystical liturgist travels from faith to love. We are being made fit receptacles for the joy held in store for us.

Human beings are made for eternal life, which is different from everlasting life. The latter means a process going on, and on, and on; the former means full, active, and conscious participation in the life of the Eternal One, and as such, it can already begin. Though we must wait to pass through the gate of death to begin everlasting life, we can already begin our eternal life. The Desert Fathers spoke of a first resurrection of the soul that occurs when we have overcome the

---

[34] Ludwig Wittgenstein, *Culture and Value* (Chicago: University of Chicago Press, 1980), 33e.

passions and aligned our will to love God above all things; a second resurrection of the body is to follow. If things work correctly, we go to our death already resurrected. There is a happiness that comes from loving, and it is different from any other sort of happiness because it is a foretaste of resurrected life. Love that makes us happy lifts us out of things temporal and points us, like an arrow, toward eternity. Most people know it when they feel it, because when they are deeply in love it is as if their toes are touching bedrock, even if otherwise they float along through life. Often this begins without any religious context, but it is already becoming a person's first contact with God.

Third, mystical belief in the resurrection may be called *hope*. We receive a different understanding of hope if love and faith coinhere. It becomes sturdier than a mild wishing for something and is actually desire awakened by love.[35] The Christian belief in the resurrection requires the theological virtue of hope, a type of hoping that Jean Daniélou says is more challenging than our ordinary understanding of the word.

> The most difficult theological virtue is hope. In spite of the promises of Christ, how many Christians there are who haven't the slightest certainty that they will one day enter into possession of the beatific vision and the overflowing joy of God! How many Christians there are who live without the conviction that they are moving toward this joy! And these people thus show little disposition to generosity because lacking certainty about what is to come, one would rather, as they say, get the most out of this life.[36]

Daniélou's words contain a truce between liturgy and social justice, between the tabernacle and the soup kitchen, between mystics and the Matthew 25 Christians. Of course we are on guard against being

---

[35] Our regular idea of faith is often so connected to a rational exercise that we can be misled. My sister-in-law had Down's syndrome and could only receive fairly limited catechesis in propositional form, but the Sunday after she died I heard these words in the Eucharistic prayer differently: "Remember also our brothers and sisters who have fallen asleep in the hope of the resurrection." I have no doubt that Kathy had fallen asleep in the hope of the resurrection—that was the form her faith took.

[36] Jean Daniélou, *Prayer: Mission of the Church* (Grand Rapids, MI: Eerdmans, 1996), 7.

so heavenly-minded that we're of no earthly good, but that needn't be a danger, because the very accomplishment of a liturgical celebration of the mystery of the resurrection floods the light of hope into our hearts, which produces generosity. It is the person who does *not* hope, and is tethered to temporality, who concludes he might as well eat, drink, and be merry if this really is all there is. If we are really only flickering bits of consciousness that will be snuffed out tomorrow, we might as well focus on the little pleasure we can squeeze out of today. (How simple life must be for a hedonist!) But hope in the resurrection allows us to take the proper measure of our brief time in this world, and this does not make us neglect our neighbor, it stirs up greater generosity. We have seen this in the lives of many mystics. The saint with a soul soaring upward into heaven does not forget the world; to the contrary, he or she is in the most radically free position to transform it. Chesterton said his first attractions to Christianity came when he realized that Christians were the only ones to preach the paradox that one must be "enough of a pagan to die for the world, and enough of a Christian to die to it."[37] Hope allows us to love the world radically, without practical calculation or cost analysis. Hope gives courage. Hope gives fortitude. Hope lets us love recklessly.

In conclusion, the triplet name for the subjective state required to believe in the resurrection is derived from the theological virtues: faith–love–hope. It is a mystical state and is therefore more than human belief, human affection, and human confidence. It is Christ's faith in the Father, Christ's love for the Father, and Christ's hope in the Father formed into a *habitus* for us by the Holy Spirit. The subjective state required for belief in the resurrection comes from mystical union with him, contracted in the liturgical mysteries. Then the three theological virtues hold hands. In his little classic *Portal of the Mystery of Hope,* Charles Péguy imagines faith, hope, and love as three sisters. Faith and love are older; hope is the youngest and smallest of the three.

> The little hope moves forward in between her two older
> sisters and one
> scarcely notices her.
> On the path to salvation, on the earthly path, on the rocky

---

[37] G. K. Chesterton, *Orthodoxy,* in *G. K. Chesterton Collected Works,* vol. 1 (San Francisco: Ignatius Press, 1986), 275.

path of
salvation, on the interminable road, on the road in be-
tween
her two older sisters, the little hope
Pushes on. . . .
And no one pays attention, the Christian people don't pay
attention,
except to the two older sisters.
[But] It's she, the little one, who carries them all.
Because Faith sees only what is.
But she, she sees what will be.
Charity loves only what is.
But she, she loves what will be.[38]

Hope can see what will be, and therefore empowers both faith and charity. To become certain of the resurrection would require more than a movement of the mind; it would also require a movement of the heart. Pascal points out that path to belief: "Endeavour, then, to convince yourself, not by increase of proofs of God, but by the abatement of your passions."[39] To know the certainty of resurrection, the virtues of faith, hope, and love must co-inhere like a conceptual perichoresis.

Faith dares *hope* that divine *love* will go to the lengths it has gone. This is the mystic confidence we seek. When Satan burgled Eden, he took the most valuable possession in it, which was not some object in the garden but rather its inhabitant. And Satan thought he had a stronghold in which to secure Adam. He could hide man from God by shame and accusation and death. He took Adam to a place he thought was out of God's reach. But he was mistaken, as Ephrem the Syrian sings in his *Hymns on Paradise*:

Adam was heedless
as guardian of Paradise,
for the crafty thief
stealthily entered;
leaving aside the fruit

---

[38] Charles Péguy, *The Portal of the Mystery of Hope* (Grand Rapids, MI: Eerdmans, 1996), 10–11.
[39] Blaise Pascal, *Pensees* (New York: E. P. Dutton, 1958), 68.

—which most men would covet—
he stole instead
the Garden's inhabitant!
Adam's Lord came out to seek him;
He entered Sheol and found him there,
then led and brought him out
to set him once more in Paradise.[40]

When the man and the woman hid themselves from the presence of the Lord God among the trees of the garden, the Lord God called, saying, "Where are you?" (Gen 3:9). The cry, "Adam, Eve, where are you?" sounded in the garden for the first time. Then angels went to the corners of the universe shouting the question, not only because they were bid by their Lord to do so, but also because they missed the human voice in the celestial choir. The King sent inquisitors with the question through the long corridors of history—Abraham, Moses, Elijah, Isaiah—but neither could they find Adam and Eve. Finally, the Lord put on flesh, so that he could die, so that he could look in the last, last place. And there, in Sheol, he found them: deaf, mute, ashamed, dead. And the Lord brought out the man and woman and led them once more to paradise. This dogma is written in icon, too.[41]

This is what we celebrate every eighth day in every liturgy, which is why Kavanagh would say that Sunday is not a small Easter, Easter is a big Sunday. This transfiguring, faithful, loving, and hopeful belief in the resurrection is nurtured there, at the foot of the ambo that declares our promised beatitude, and at the foot of the altar where we celebrate the Paschal reorientation of our existence to life. We are directed to the time when we will slough off our garments of skin and be arrayed in glory. Clothing and re-clothing is a Christian image of the resurrection, and well described by Claudel: "This flick of the nail which will split our pod from top to bottom. . . . Our material body yellows and withers until the seed of immortality is ready."[42] It was not made to last forever in its present form. "This body which we have inherited through a series of intersecting accidents is now rightfully

---

[40] Ephrem the Syrian, *Hymns on Paradise* (Crestwood, NY: Saint Vladimir's Seminary Press, 1990), 135.

[41] Quoting myself in *Theologia Prima: What Is Liturgical Theology?* (Chicago: Hillenbrand Books, 2004), 29–30.

[42] Claudel, *I Believe in God*, 267.

ours through grace,"[43] but one day it will be glorified. "The soul therefore surrenders her old tunic to the elements while waiting to be reclothed in that new and innocent garment which He has promised."[44] Our heavenly garments will be white, like light. We will *be* light. We will be splendored in beauty by truth with goodness. "This is the stuff of our baptismal gown. . . . This is the cloth which heaven supplies to the wardrobe of the Holy Father. This is the linen closet where we would like to plunge our arms and draw forth those noble fabrics with which we would clothe ourselves in folds of glory!"[45] The resurrection to come will be the Great Spring when we will slough off our mortality, the Final Spring when we will discover that our garments of clay are capable of moving with spiritual agility. But already we begin to stretch our limbs, as Cabasilas said of the fetal saint.

To realize that we are made for eternity radically reorients our priorities: we are turned to the East and see each moment through the mystical lens of an impending resurrection. Here is Gregory of Nyssa on how to protect what is below by placing our eyes on what is above:

> This is the safest way to protect the good things you enjoy: by realizing how much your Creator has honored you above all creatures. He did not make the heavens in his image, nor the moon, the sun, the beauty of the stars, nor anything else which you can see in the created universe. You alone are made in the likeness of that nature which surpasses all understanding; you alone are a similitude of eternal beauty, a receptacle of happiness, an image of the true Light. . . . All the heavens fit into the palm of God's hand; the earth and sea are measured in the hollow of his hand. And though he is so great that he can grasp all creation in his palm, you can wholly embrace him; he dwells within you, nor is he cramped as he pervades your entire being.
>
> If you realize this you will not allow your eye to rest on anything of this world. Indeed, you will no longer marvel even at the heavens. For how can you admire the heavens, my [child], when you see that you are more permanent than they?

---

43 Claudel, *I Believe in God*, 268.
44 Claudel, *I Believe in God*, 269.
45 Claudel, *I Believe in God*, 305.

For the heavens pass away, but you will abide for all eternity with Him who is forever.[46]

The theological virtues of faith, hope, and love make us into people who share Eternal Life with the Eternal One, and our vocation is to be witnesses of that in the valley of death—martyrs of the resurrection—where we currently toil. Resurrection life is trampling down death by death, as the Byzantine Paschal troparion sings throughout the Easter season. It is the liturgical song on the lips of liturgical mystics. Each of the saints reveal another facet of what resurrection life looks like, which is why we like to keep their company. Though space, time, and matter will evanesce, we are capable of being made into a three-sided liturgical loom on which eternal life is woven, one day to be gently lifted off by the master weaver, without dropping a stitch, and fitted into his own radiant garment. The sepulcher becomes a birth canal.

---

[46] Gregory of Nyssa, *From Glory to Glory: Texts from Gregory of Nyssa's Mystical Writings*, comp. Jean Daniélou (Crestwood, NY: St. Vladimir's Seminary Press, 1979), 162–163.

CHAPTER 6

THE PATHWAY HOME

Now something quite remarkable has happened, but did we even notice it slip by? As is so often the case when grace perfects nature, it happens so stealthily that we hardly notice that things have been put aright and we've been rescued. Mysticism has passed through the purification of asceticism to produce a grammar of liturgical theology that is different from the grammar spoken by the philosophers. Most of the history of philosophy has understood the three dichotomies that Gregory the Great named (inward–outward, above–below, then–now) as antagonistic to one another, and understandably so because there is a tension here. I have, myself, included an element of tension in my expressions up to this point. But now liturgical theology lets us speak with a new language, a new formal grammar shaped by the liturgy, a new logic coming from the Logos, causing an unanticipated effect upon the mind that is undergoing conversion. Now suddenly, unexpectedly, everything speaks of God. Everything points to God. The world receives a luminosity and becomes a theophany. Under the spell of liturgical mysticism, peace is made within the triad of pairs we have been using from Gregory. In liturgy's contact with mysticism, liturgical theology can reestablish harmony between the outward and inward, between our home below and heaven above, between the present moment and the eschaton coming. The former realities (outward, below, now) no longer combat the latter realities (inward, above, to come), but instead the former awaken an appetite for the latter. And why should this not be so?

Everything else in creation possesses a teleological ought: the seed ought to sprout, the branch ought to bloom, the flower ought to bear fruit. We ourselves ought to pass from childhood to youth, and youth to adulthood, so why is it surprising that biological life ought to pass forward to mystical life? Paul Claudel said, "It seems as if the acorn knows its destiny and carries within itself an active idea of the oak required of it."[1]

Let us assume that our love for God is a kind of appetite. That mystical appetite can go wrong in two ways, and the first needs correction by liturgical asceticism and the second needs correction by liturgical theology. After that, outward things now below can lead us inward to things above still to come.

First, our appetites can go wrong for not being consistent and ruled. We live within a welter of stimulation upon both our bodies and minds. Our bodies are bombarded by stimulations of sights and sounds drifting into our senses, our muscles weary, and our nerves are excited by pains and pleasures. Our minds also are bombarded by stimulations, as memories are evoked by a passing sight or sound, imaginations project us into the future, and we experience emotional responses to what is going on around us. In both body and soul, the human person is the matrix of a thousand bits of data input. How do we handle that? Some people change in order to accommodate the flux of sensations, as quickly as a chameleon will change colors to match a constantly changing background. But if we do that, are we not the slaves of our changing appetites, instead of master of them? If we fail to direct our appetites, do we not thereby fail to cultivate a life with teleological orientation toward mysticism's final beatitude? The beatific life requires a sort of integrity from us, from *integer*, meaning whole and complete: integrity means being a person who wants, instead of a person who is a collection of wants. Holmer thinks it requires a kind of attentiveness. "If someone says, 'My trouble is I've never known what I wanted,' the issue is not the hiddenness and internal privacy of wants, but very probably that one has never wanted steadily and long. The problem is not that my 'wants' are unknowable, even to me; the problem is that I have not trained my wants, like I have not trained my eye on the target. Failing this, there is no 'I.'"[2] Who we are is partly composed by what we have

---

[1] Paul Claudel, *The Essence of the Bible* (New York: Philosophical Library, 1957), 64.

[2] Paul Holmer, "Post-Kierkegaard: Remarks About Being a Person" (unpublished manuscript, 1981).

loved long and hard, and if we let our loves flit like a nervous sparrow from chocolate bars to Netflix to English literature to Greek poetry to soccer to the next promotion, then we will have become nothing but a collage of magazine ads with no real person underneath. We will have let our desire dissipate, like water will spread over acres of land once outside the riverbanks. So Holmer continues, "If one's subjectivity is made up only of episodic and trivial desires, stimulated by accident and circumstance, then one is not a person at all. No self gets a chance to develop."[3] Claudel describes that kind of life, too:

> How long is it that we have just been jogging along, just jogging along? How long have we been piling up inside us, stuffing inside us like soiled linen in a suitcase, one on top of the other, anyhow, things, people, memories, wishes, impressions, books, talks, opinions, successes, failures, humiliations, vices, good deeds, bad deeds: and the worst of it is that they are not dead things, they are all alive and kicking and wriggling and talking and grunting and shunting and trying painfully to fit in with one another and attending to orders coming from outside with the most artificial pauses or poses. We know all too well what happens on sleepless nights, for instance, when the whole lot starts stirring and pushing and screaming at once.[4]

Actually, we will only have a kind of consistency or texture to our lives if we want steadily and long, and only if we want worthwhile things, and only if we judge between the trivial and the consequential, and only if we focus our attention so as to order the mass of sensations.

There is a second way our appetites can go wrong. The first way was to not want long and steadily, to not tie ourselves to a desire or a goal long enough for that object to control our subjectivity, and that is why the appetite must be corrected by a discipline, training, and askesis. But the second way for our appetites to fail is if they are directed toward the wrong end, even if they are done steadfastly. The first book C. S. Lewis wrote after his conversion to Christianity was an allegorical tale titled *The Pilgrim's Regress*. The protagonist, John, thinks he is running away from the Landlord and toward a distant is-

---

[3] Paul Holmer, "Post-Kierkegaard."

[4] Paul Claudel, *Lord, Teach Us to Pray* (London: Dennis Dobson, 1942), 8.

land that became his heart's desire from the first moment he glimpsed it through the window and exclaimed, "I know now what I want." But John is easily distracted by other desires and fears, and the whole allegory consists of almost forgetting the Island by indulging in all sorts of other desires, for all sorts of other things, for all the wrong reasons. Yet, after experiencing each counterfeit desire he says, "If it's what I wanted, why am I so disappointed when I get it?" and the reason why is finally explained by Mr. Wisdom:

> *What does not satisfy when we find it, was not the thing we were desiring.* If water will not set a man at ease, then be sure it was not thirst, or not thirst only, that tormented him. . . . How, indeed, do we know our desires save by their satisfaction? When do we know them until we say, "Ah, *this* is what I wanted"? And if there were any desire which it was natural for man to feel but impossible for man to satisfy, would not the nature of this desire remain to him always ambiguous?[5]

If what is outward, below, and now does not satisfy when we attain it, then it is not the thing we truly desire.

This is a predicament each man and woman bears from the wound of the original sin of Adam and Eve, and must be rectified by a theology that possesses knowledge of what happiness will please us, what beatitude we were made for, what liturgical *telos* will finally fit us. Not just any old end will do. The worthiness of the desire should be called forth from the object, and not merely the subject's conviction, as Holmer told us: in latria the object, not the subject, calls forth the proper kind of worship. A "greater appetite" or "superior desire" is not measured on a subjective Richter scale of how much the earth moves when we have our reactions, it is measured by where the loved object is located on the scale of being. To have an enthusiasm for something is neither surprising nor does it make us commendable; the question is whether we *should* have a passion for the thing. Is the thing worthy of the desire? Are we better, happier, and purer people for desiring the thing? This is an examination to which liturgical theology subjects us. Because God is the highest being, God should receive the highest love, with the greatest desire. Our love for God is the highest love in our life because God is the highest reality to be loved. In one way,

---

[5] C. S. Lewis, *The Pilgrim's Regress* (London: Fount Paperbacks, 1977), 163.

this is natural, because the image of God has never been completely effaced, but in another way, it demands a difficult choice of each one of us. We must choose our loves carefully.

St. Thomas observes that "[a]ll the powers of the soul are left, as it were, destitute of their proper order, whereby they are naturally directed to virtue; which destitution is called a wounding of nature."[6] We are created with faculties or abilities that are unique to human beings, faculties that are "powers of the soul" and not possessed by animals in the same manner, and each of them is a conduit to one of the four cardinal virtues. When our muscles are properly flexed, our legs are animated and we can walk; when our love is properly flexed, our lives are animated and we can walk with an upright life. But there has been a displacement, like a bone out of its socket. We don't do nature naturally any more, and an unnatural (misdirected) love is a vice. What Thomas goes on to say is elucidated by John Adam Moehler's translation.

> All the faculties of the soul have been, to a certain degree, displaced from their proper direction and destination—a displacement which is called the wound of nature. But there are four powers of the soul, which can become the conduits of virtue—namely, reason, wherein is recognition; the will, wherein is justice; the faculty of exertion, wherein is courage; the faculty of desire, wherein is temperance. In so far as reason has been diverted from its bearing towards the truth, has arisen the wound of ignorance; inasmuch as the will has been diverted from its bearing towards good, has arisen the wound of wickedness; inasmuch as the faculty of exertion has been diverted from its bearing towards the arduous, has arisen the wound of frailty; lastly, inasmuch as the faculty of desire has been diverted from its course, as directed by reason, towards the term of pleasure, has arisen concupiscence.[7]

The intellect, the will, strength, and the desire must work in synergy. The intellect must train the appetites under the rulership of their

---

6 Thomas Aquinas, *ST* II-I, q. 85, a. 3 (968).

7 John Adam Mohler, *Symbolism: Or, Exposition of the Doctrinal Differences Between Catholics and Protestants as Evidenced by Their Symbolical Writings* (London: Gibbings, 1906), 50.

teleological ought so they settle on the right things. Only then is the spell of worldliness broken, and only then does our roving eye alight upon its true satisfaction.

How each person comes to this moment of crisis is private to that person and God. But common to each experience of spell-breaking is the repaired integration of our interior life with our exterior activity, of heavenly desire with earthly vocation, of the eternal pressing upon our temporal life (inward–outward, above–below, then–now). To be startled into training our eyes upon what is inward, above, and to come is a constant process of conversion, but the failure of what is outward, below, and going on now can contribute to that realization, as Lewis discovered.

> If I find in myself a desire which no experience in this world can satisfy, the most probable explanation is that I was made for another world. If none of my earthly pleasures satisfy it, that does not prove that the universe is a fraud. Probably earthly pleasures were never meant to satisfy it, but only to arouse it, to suggest the real thing. . . . I must keep alive in myself the desire for my true country, which I shall not find till after death; I must never let it get snowed under or turned aside; I must make it the main object of life to press on to that other country and to help others to do the same.[8]

A bow properly strung, and an arrow properly aimed, can hit the target of mystical happiness, but this will never happen with a dissipated, unstrung desire that has gone limp (the first way desire can fail), or with an arrow aimed at a wrong mark (the second way desire can fail). The taut bow and the archer's eye must work together to hit the target; liturgical asceticism and liturgical theology must work together, guiding our desires, in order to reach liturgical mysticism. A conversion under grace will ascetically equip us for a latria that guides our comprehension of the world and disciplines the desires the world stimulates in us. Seeing the world in the mystery of the resurrection re-conditions our estimate of the world so that we can do it the way it was meant to be done (liturgically).

And then the remarkable thing, that we hardly noticed slip by, will

---

[8] C. S. Lewis, *Mere Christianity*, in *The Complete C. S. Lewis Signature Classics* (San Francisco: HarperSanFrancisco, 2007), 114.

have happened. Then the world will no longer sidetrack us from God, it will become a pathway to God. Gregory himself, the very author of our three paired tensions, admits as much. Here are several examples:

- Our present life is the road by which we journey on to our home: and we are harassed here by frequent disturbances, in the secret judgment of God, expressly that we may not love our road instead of our home.[9]
- "House" is for resting place, and "path" for conduct. A path therefore leads to a house, because our doings lead onto our resting place.[10]
- What is signified by Job but the life of the good that are married who, while they do deeds of mercy by the good things of the world which they possess, do it as it were advanced to their heavenly country by the paths of the earth?[11]
- The soul, thrusting aside the bodily form, is brought to the knowledge of itself. . . . And by thus thinking of itself to prepare itself a pathway to contemplate the substance of Eternity.[12]

There is no sin in being on the pathway; the spiritualists are wrong. But there is a sin in loving our road instead of our home; the materialists are wrong. There is no sin in being on the road, in being corporeal, in being finite, in being *homo viator*, in having responsibility for things outside, below, and now; there is only sin in settling for the lesser, and not letting it awaken an appetite for the greater.

Duality must not be misread as dualism. Dualism is a lie, and every lie can be traced to its original source, Satan, the Liar who acts diabolically, which means to throw apart in different directions (*dia-ballein*). What is diabolical is fissured, and such is the state Satan has chosen for himself vis-à-vis God and into which he malevolently wishes to draw us. He beguiled our parents by withholding the fact that God would have given them the fruit from both trees had they remained obedient. He beguiles us, too, by withholding the fact that obedience does not mean loss of freedom, as we are inclined to think.

---

[9] Gregory the Great, *Moralia in Job*, vol. 3 (n.p.: Ex Fontibus, 2012), 41.
[10] Gregory the Great, *Moralia in Job*, 3:301.
[11] Gregory the Great, *Moralia in Job*, vol. 1 (n.p.: Ex Fontibus, 2012), 41.
[12] Gregory the Great, *Moralia in Job*, 1:266.

When the tempter said, "Did God say, 'You shall not eat of any tree of the garden'?" (Gen 3:1), Adam and Eve should have answered, "Yes we can! Look at all the trees we may eat from! They are all for us. But that one tree only, that one single tree, we must not eat from yet, because if we take it too early, without preparation and permission, then we will die. We must not eat from that tree in any other way but in obedience that expresses our love." But the tempter turns the prohibition into a doubt and then into a dare: "Is God holding out on you? And if he is holding out on you, should you perhaps withhold your sacrifice of obedience to him?"

If I may indulge using C. S. Lewis one more time, I will recall a scene from the second novel in his science fiction trilogy, titled *Perelandra*. He retells the story of Genesis, only this time the Fall is avoided. The characters involved are a human being named Ransom, a human being named Weston who is possessed by the devil, and the Green Lady, Queen of this world, its Eve. Maleldil (God) has given the commandment that on this watery planet the Lady should return to one of the floating islands each night and not spend it on fixed land, so that is exactly the commandment the devil tries to make her break, speaking through the possessed Weston. First, he argues that unless she disobeys this commandment, she will not become "older," which he claims is exactly what Maleldil wishes for her, and what she will only attain if she acts out of her own autonomy. Second, he suggests this law is arbitrary. Since he has been to other planets and not seen it applied anywhere else, she is free to disobey it because it is not universal. To mount a counter argument, Ransom must propose another reason for why this law is different from all others.

> I think He made one law of that kind in order that there might be obedience. In all these other matters what you call obeying Him is but doing what seems good in your own eyes also. Is love content with that? You do them, indeed, because they are His will, but not only because they are His will. Where can you taste the joy of obeying unless He bids you do something for which His bidding is the *only* reason? When we spoke last you said that if you told the beasts to walk on their heads, they would delight to do so. So I know that you understand well what I am saying.[13]

---

[13] C. S. Lewis, *Perelandra* (New York: Scribner, 1972), 101.

In other words—my words, trying to apply this passage to our topic— in every act wherein I love God, I also benefit. As Thomas Aquinas admits, "[W]e do not offend God except by doing something contrary to our own good."[14] When God says, "Do not covet," it is like saying, "Don't play in the street." Every commandment we obey serves our own good, except one that feels different because it is not commanded for our protection, it is presented as an opportunity for self-gift (i.e., the joy of obeying).

And the Lady's reaction?

> "Oh, brave [Ransom]," said the Green Lady, "this is the best you have said yet. This makes me older far: yet it does not feel like the oldness this other is giving me. Oh, how well I see it! We cannot walk out of Maleldil's will: but He has given us a way to walk out of *our* will. And there could be no such way except a command like this. Out of our own will. It is like passing out through the world's roof into Deep Heaven. All beyond is love Himself. I knew there was joy in looking upon the Fixed Island and laying down all thought of ever living there, but I did not till now understand."[15]

The Green Lady has discovered a new reason, a new desire, a new mind, which shows her a way to walk out of her own will. This commandment exists so that by keeping it she can take hold of a hand extended to her in love. The joy to be had in keeping this type of law is a joy known only to lovers—to spouses, to parents, to friends, and especially to that triune fellowship of lovers: it is the joy of obedience, of being in right hierarchy. The Son's total delight is to do what his Father tells him. When Satan tempted him in the wilderness to do his own will by turning the stones into bread, his reply was simply that he would rather live from every word of his Father than from bread alone. As the Green Lady found joy in looking at the Fixed Land but laid down all thought of living there, Christ found joy in looking upon the stones and laying down all thought of making them bread because that was not his Father's will.

The Fall was an act disobedience, so the reversal of that fall re-

---

[14] Thomas Aquinas, *Summa Contra Gentiles* (Notre Dame: University of Notre Dame Press, 1975), III.122.2.

[15] C. S. Lewis, *Perelandra*, 101–102.

quires a radical act of obedience if mankind is to resume its ascent to heaven. We get a glimpse of that kind of obedience in Jesus, who always lived in his Father's will; in Mary's fiat; in saints who have made their will pliable by prayer, fasting, and almsgiving. Liturgical fasting trains us for a radically free and mystical obedience. Man was not made for outward, earthly, and temporal bread alone; men and women were made with capacities for the eternal. Latria will lift our eyes in a liturgy that does not express how we see things, but rather proposes, instead, how God sees all things. The sacramental symbolism of Christian liturgy can become the alphabet of the vocabulary in the dialogue revealing the hypostatic union. Christ is the primordial mystery of God in the flesh, and the sacraments (which are his symbols) and the Church (which is his fundamental sacrament) perpetuate the Incarnation, which assumes manhood into God.

Adam disobeyed in a garden, the New Adam obeyed in a desert; the command was a constraint for Adam, fulfilling the command was a joy for the New Adam; Adam had plenty to eat and still hungered for the one forbidden thing, the New Adam had nothing to eat but hungered for only one thing. Schmemann writes, "[T]he 'original' sin is not primarily that man has 'disobeyed' God; the sin is that he ceased to be hungry for God and God alone. . . . The only real fall of man is his noneucharistic life in a noneucharistic world."[16] The story of salvation can be told as a story of appetites—lost, restored, and cultivated: the Garden of Eden, the grace of manna, Jesus's forty days, the Eucharist, the Messianic banquet. It is a desire (theology) that must be disciplined (asceticism) so that it is constant (liturgy) and directed toward the right object (mysticism), because what does not satisfy when we find it was not the thing we were desiring. Man does not live by bread alone.

God's response to Satan's lies was to send the Truth in the flesh, splendoring, a man who was beautiful for glorifying his Father, a liturgical man. Olivier Clément writes,

> In Christ the world is joined together again in symbol, in a profusion of symbols. The invisible part appears in the visible: the visible draws its meaning from the invisible. . . . God transcends the intelligible as well as the visible, but through

---

[16] Alexander Schmemann, *For the Life of the World* (Crestwood, NY: St. Vladimir's Seminary Press, 1973), 18.

the incarnation of the Logos he penetrates them both, trans-figures and unites them. The world is a vast incarnation which the fall of the human race tries to contradict. The *diabolos*, the opposite of the *symbolon*, is continually trying to keep apart the separated halves of the ring; but they come together in Christ. Christian symbolism expresses nothing less than the union in Christ of the divine and the human—of which the cosmos becomes the dialogue—displaying the circulation in Christ of glory between 'earth' and 'heaven,' between the visible and the invisible.[17]

The quotation makes two facts clear about the pattern in Gregory's pairs. First, Clément says *the invisible part appears in the visible.* Therefore, with our new mind we can discern the inward appearing in the outward, determine what is above appearing in what is below, and discover that what shall come is already working on us. Second, he says *the visible draws its meaning from the invisible.* Therefore our new mind can discern that pattern, too: the outward discovers its meaning from the inward, what is below makes greater sense in light of what is above, and the present can be understood by its terminus. Human beings are hybrid worshippers (Gregory Nazianzus), microcosms and mediators (Gregory of Nyssa), and man and woman can carry out their liturgical function as cosmic priests only when the symbolism of the cosmos is restored. When we carry out that liturgical function, then we have the taste of the mystical on our lips. We can taste mystery when liturgy, theology, and asceticism are reintegrated.

The key requirement is that we not confuse the pathway with the house. We require clarity on this point above all others if truth, goodness, and beauty are to operate mystically in us. The virtue of *truth* can lead to eternal Truth only if we do not stop on the way, satisfied with a temporary truth, or an incomplete historical narrative, or an empirical equation. The virtue of *goodness* can lead to the One who is truly good only if we do not content ourselves with a restricted morality and a situational ethic. And the virtue of *beauty* can lead to Infinite Beauty only if we do not settle for fading glories and a handsomeness that will decay. C. S. Lewis sighs aloud, "It would seem that Our Lord finds our desires not too strong, but too weak. We are half-heart-

---

[17] Olivier Clément, *The Roots of Christian Mysticism* (Hyde Park, NY: New City Press, 1996), 219.

ed creatures, fooling about with drink and sex and ambition when infinite joy is offered us, like an ignorant child who wants to go on making mud pies in a slum because he cannot imagine what is meant by the offer of a holiday at the sea. We are far too easily pleased."[18] We half-hearted creatures must be taught not to be too easily pleased with the pathway, even while it can please us as we progress.

That is why the philosophers, if they were sane philosophers, were correct in feeling the tension they mistook for dualism, the tension between soul and body, spirit and matter. They were correct because they sensed that mankind is far too easily pleased. However, no matter how sound was their judgment in the diagnosis, they could not by reason alone have guessed the cure, because the cure was a novel act undertaken by God's sovereign decision. According to Paul, the mystery in the mind of the Father from all eternity could only be revealed by an action of God in history. To the Colossians he says the mystery has been "hidden for ages and generations" (Col 1:26), and he writes to the Ephesians to "make all men see what is the plan of the mystery hidden for ages in God, who created all things" (Eph 3:9). In God's mysterious plan, the Father "chose us in [Christ] before the foundation of the world. . . . [And] destined us in love to be his sons through Jesus Christ, according to the purpose of his will" (Eph 1:4–5). The mystery is that we were created to give latria by the authority of the Holy Spirit empowering us.

The good of man and woman is not to be found on the pathway, it is only to be found in their final home—except nobody knew how high a home God had planned for mankind! And that, exclaims John Chrysostom, is exactly the mystery.

> Strange! What Friendship! For [God] tells us His secrets; the mysteries . . . of his will, as if one should say, He has made known to us *the things that are in His heart*. For here is indeed the mystery which is full of all wisdom and prudence. . . . [T]his He desired, this He travailed for, as one might say, that He might be able to reveal to us the mystery. What mystery? That He would have man seated up on high. And this has come to pass.[19]

---

[18] C. S. Lewis, "The Weight of Glory," in *The Weight of Glory* (San Francisco: HarperSanFrancisco, 2007), 26.

[19] John Chrysostom, Homily 1 on Ephesians 1:1–3, in *Nicene and Post-Nicene Fa-*

What is liturgical mysticism's aim? To be seated up on high. Who can discover that this pathway of truth, beauty, and goodness—even though it passes through the valley of the shadow of death—leads ultimately to that end? The baptized liturgist. What does the resurrected soul discover when the world is done the way it was meant to be done? That what is inward, below, and given for present enjoyment is only a pathway to this seat on high. Human beings will not find fulfillment short of the end to which liturgical mysticism witnesses, and this is the fundamental evangelical function of the Church. The Church exists for the purpose of proclaiming to every living person that they are made for adoption as coheirs with Christ, and this evangelism is liturgical in nature because liturgy already gives us an experience of our home mystery by drawing the future into the present in such a way that the eschaton is not simply a "not yet."

Liturgy is served by asceticism by keeping our senses healthy, and liturgy is served by mysticism by keeping a shy, persistent inner voice whispering in us. Asceticism pushes, mysticism pulls. Like a salmon swimming upstream, our liturgy is pushed and pulled up the great liturgical river of divine energies flowing from the throne of God and the Lamb. Jean Corbon has navigated that river's headwaters. "Here we find life in its eternal outpouring: the river of life, which John contemplates at the heart of history, is an energy of love at work before the world was. Yes, the mysterious river of divine communion is an outpouring of love among the Three, and in it eternal life consists. . . . This river, this energy, is wholly other: it is the self-opening of our thrice holy God."[20] The perichoresis of the Trinity has been kenotically extended.

Plato did not know to what lengths God might go in order to heal this sickness unto death, and we cannot blame him for that since he lived before Year One. The Greeks found it foolishness and the Jews a scandal, and even the angels were astonished at the sight when they peered into the stable at Bethlehem. Coventry Patmore describes what Plato got right, and then what Plato missed, in one of his most brilliant entries in *The Rod, the Root, and the Flower*. First, what Plato got right:

thers, vol. 13, First Series, *Chrysostom: Homilies on Galatians, Ephesians, Philippians, Colossians, Thessalonians, Timothy, Titus, and Philemon*, ed. Philip Schaff (Peabody, Massachusetts: Hendrickson, 2004), 53. Emphases added.
[20] Jean Corbon, *The Wellspring of Worship* (New York: Paulist Press, 1988), 16.

Plato's cave of shadows is the most profound and simple statement of the relation of the natural to the spiritual life ever
made. Men stand with their backs to the Sun, and they take
the shadows cast by it upon the walls of their cavern for realities. The shadows, even, of heavenly realities are so alluring
as to provoke ardent desires, but they cannot satisfy us. They
mock us with unattainable good, and our natural and legiti-
mate passions and instincts, in the absence of their true and
substantial satisfactions, break forth into frantic disorders. If
we want fruition we must turn our backs on the shadows, and
gaze on their realities in God.[21]

This mockery and franticness animates most pagan mysticism. Most
pagan mysticism wishes to turn from unsatisfying shadows to ecstatic
satisfactions. Liturgical mysticism differs from other types of mysticism because it possesses something the other mysticisms are missing.
Patmore continues:

It may be added that, when we have done this, and are weary
of the splendours and felicities of immediate reality, we may
turn again, from time to time, to the shadows, which, having
thus become intelligible, and being attributed by us to their
true origin, are immeasurably more satisfying than they were
before, and may be delighted in without blame. This is the
"evening joy," the joy of contemplating God in His creatures,
of which the theologians write; and this purified and intelligible joy in the shadow—which has now obtained a core of
substance—is not only the hundredfold "promise of this life
also," but it is, as the Church teaches, a large part of the joy
of the blest.[22]

I think that Evagrius's second stage, physike, could be called this
evening joy. After the shadows's turmoil is tamed by liturgical asceticism, liturgical theology can do the world the way it was meant
to be done, and mysticism can delight without blame in the *outward*

---

[21] Coventry Patmore, *The Rod, the Root, and the Flower* (London: George Bell and
Sons, 1895), 68. I also made this point in *Consecrating the World* (New York: Angelico Press, 2016), 22–23.
[22] Patmore, *The Rod*, 68–69.

things *present* even here *below*. The tensions Gregory named have been healed. Ascetical mysticism plays liturgical theology in an erotic key by stirring a thirst for truth, beauty, and goodness in a transformed mind that can only be slaked when man's eros has been purified and straightened in its trajectory. Now anything *outside* will drive us further in to find God, anything *below* will drive us further up to find God, anything that happens *now* will drive us onward to find God. The beatific vision beckons from the foretaste we have of it at the Mass.

This liturgical mysticism does something to the sacraments, too. If you taste and see, you will see that you have not tasted enough yet. The sacraments are not designed to fulfill our appetites, they are designed to increase those appetites. The sacraments should not satisfy us, they should increase our thirst. Thus Symeon the New Theologian writes, "I always thirst, although in my mouth there is always some water";[23] Bernard of Clairvaux says that "only he who drinks still thirsts for more";[24] and Catherine of Siena writes that

> You, Eternal Trinity, are a deep-sea: the more I enter you, the more I discover, and the more I discover, the more I seek you. You are insatiable, you in whose depth the soul is sated yet remains always hungry for you, thirsty for you, Eternal Trinity. . . . Truly this light is a sea, for it nourishes the soul in you, peaceful sea, Eternal Trinity. Its water is not sluggish, so the soul is not afraid because she knows the truth.[25]

The sacraments are only picnic lunches on the pathway, and not yet the Messianic banquet in our final home. Therefore, every sacrament should have the quality of *viaticum* to us: they are a provision of something necessary for a journey.

We should never be satisfied with our current progress on the pathway, but as I have been at pains to point out, the mysticism of which we speak does not condemn or abandon the pathway. Sometimes mysticism is described as an ecstasy that pulls a person out of

---

[23] Symeon the New Theologian, *Hymns of Divine Love* (Denville, NJ: Dimension Books, 1976), 120.

[24] Bernard of Clairvaux, *On the Song of Songs,* vol. 1 (Kalamazoo, Michigan: Cistercian Publications, 1971), 16.

[25] Catherine of Siena, *The Dialogue,* The Classics of Western Spirituality (New York: Paulist Press, 1980), 364.

this world, like a tooth is pulled out of its socket, but to the contrary, liturgical mysticism remains concerned with the renewal of creation. Because the mysticism is liturgical, it operates in a liturgical manner, which involves mediation. Liturgy is the descent and ascent of the divine energies. In the first movement, the Spirit comes down to renew the face of the earth, and in the second movement the world's praise is raised up to the Father for his glorification. These two movements occur through Jesus the Mediator, the High Priest, the primordial liturgist who bore his blood into the presence of God and opened heaven through the veil of his flesh so that the liturgy of our present life may be united to his eternal liturgy. A priest is a mediator. Such mediation was a work that Adam and Eve were created to do as cosmic priests, but failed when they lost their taste for liturgy by biting into the forbidden fruit, so now they need their mouths washed out with baptismal water.

Schmemann defines original sin as having lost our desire to be a priest, with a resultant wound inflicted upon the world when we no longer do it as it was meant to be done (viz., sacramentally and sacrificially).

> The natural dependence of man upon the world was intended to be transformed constantly into communion with God in whom is all life. Man was to be the priest of a eucharist, offering the world to God. . . . The world is meaningful only when it is the "sacrament" of God's presence. Things treated merely as things in themselves destroy themselves because only in God have they any life. The world of nature, cut off from the source of life, is a dying world. For one who thinks food in itself is the source of life, eating is communion with the dying world, it is communion with death. Food itself is dead, it is life that has died and it must be kept in refrigerators like a corpse.[26]

We think it is normal not to be a mystic, like we think it is normal to keep dead food in a refrigerator. But it is not. It is fallen life, unnatural, abnormal. Natural life, normal life, the life that glorifies God by being fully alive (the reference is to Irenaeus) is restored to us by Christ the great High Priest whose Paschal mystery is intended to

---

[26] Schmemann, *For the Life of the World*, 17.

enter us by liturgical effect and make us, in substance, priests again. And, actually, that is the only satisfactory anthropology. Vladimir Solovyov encourages us to be something greater then we are:

> If man is only a fact, if he is inevitably limited by the mechanism of the external reality, then let him seek not anything greater than natural reality, let him 'eat, drink, and be merry.' . . . A man, however, does not wish to be a mere fact, to be only a phenomenon; in this unwillingness is already a hint that actually he is not a mere fact, that he is not a phenomenon only, but something greater. [27]

Benedict XVI associates this lost vision with the loss of our capacity for sacrament: "Initially there is no room left for that symbolic transparency of reality toward the eternal on which the sacramental principle is based."[28] He contrasts two understandings of the world, one symbolic and the other functionalist.

> Oversimplifying somewhat, one could indeed say that the sacramental idea presupposes a symbolist understanding of the world, whereas the contemporary understanding of the world is functionalist: it sees things merely as things, as a function of human labor and accomplishment, and given such a starting point, it is no longer possible to understand how a "thing" can become a "sacrament."[29]

If, however, a person takes a meal for more than simple biological nourishment, if he also performs this biological act rationally and spiritually, then "this man experiences in a meal the transparency of the sensible toward the spiritual. . . . He discovers that things are more than things."[30] When things are more than things, they are mystical. When man and woman are something greater than a phenomenon, they kiss the mystical.

Liturgical mysticism is the quickening of the infused divine ener-

---

[27] Vladimir Solovyev, *Lectures on Godmanhood* (London: Dennis Dobson, 1948), 81.

[28] Benedict XVI, "The Sacramental Foundation of Christian Existence," in *Joseph Ratzinger Collected Works*, vol. 11, *Theology of the Liturgy* (San Francisco: Ignatius Press, 2014), 153–154.

[29] Benedict XVI, *Joseph Ratzinger Collected Works*, 11:154.

[30] Benedict XVI, *Joseph Ratzinger Collected Works*, 11:158.

gies that Christ bestowed at our baptism when his invisible mystical life entered us and we entered his visible mystical body. By baptism, man and woman are restored to their predestined liturgical identity, recapitulated by Christ. An extraordinary mystic is, as Kavanagh said of the vowed ascetic, nothing more or less than a virtuoso who serves the whole community as an exemplar of the stunningly normal life lived by Christians. All charisms are given for some ministry, never for private enjoyment or profit, and the ministry of the charismatic, extraordinary mystic is to light up the temple awaiting us all at the end of this present pathway. This temple awaits every baptized and re-newed soul (even those whose conversion involves baptism by desire), and the virtuosic mystic is illuminating the mystery living in that soul. Even when a mystic has an ecstatic experience, it is for the life of the world, as is all sacramental liturgy.

Man cannot live by bread alone. Men and women require purpose and meaning, as provided by every mystery that proceeds out of the mouth of God, who is the incarnate Logos that tells us we were cre-ated to enjoy the eternal life of latria with him in the Spirit. Bernard of Clairvaux says,

> Divine love leads to an unceasing search for God, to continu-al labor for Him; it bears indefatigably all trials in union with Christ; it gives a true thirst for God; it makes us run rapidly toward Him; it gives us a holy boldness and an undaunted audacity; it attaches us inseparably to God; it burns and con-sumes us with a very sweet ardor for Him; finally, in heaven, it likens us completely to Him.[31]

He has described a baptized Christian quickening to sainthood. The image of God grows into the likeness of God at last. By means of the earthly liturgy we run (inwardly, upwardly, forwardly) to join the heavenly liturgy celebrated by the High Priest in the self-obla-tion described in the Letter to the Hebrews. The *mysticism is litur-gical* because we are following Christ in all things. The *liturgy is mystical* because our transfer from Hades to the heavenly Jerusalem can be pre-experienced, anticipated, celebrated, already undergone premortem.

---

[31] Reginald Garrigou-Lagrange, *The Three Ages of the Interior Life*, vol. 2 (London: Catholic Way, 2014), 573.

To make that clear, Benedict XVI reminds us that eternal means something different from everlasting or endless. The Pope emeritus prefers Jesus's definition in John 17:3 when our Lord says eternal life is knowing the Father and the one He sent. He writes,

> "Eternal life" is not—as the modern reader might immediately assume—life after death, in contrast to this present life, which is transient and not eternal. "Eternal life" is life itself, real life, which can also be lived in the present age and is no longer challenged by physical death. This is the point: to seize "life" here and now, real life that can no longer be destroyed by anything or anyone.[32]

Such eternal life can become the substance of our existence when the mystery is distributed under sacramental veil.

Our mystical state is an equal and opposite reaction to Christ's kenosis: he sank down, and we rise up; he sank into our sin, we soar upon his righteousness; his descent into hell raises us to heaven. (Liturgy is a remarkable pulley system hanging from heaven.) The brightness of the life to come enters through the mysteries (sacraments) and dwells in our souls even now, even here. Nicholas Cabasilas uses this fact to explain why we become different while still remaining where we are:

> He did not remove us from here, but He made us heavenly while yet remaining on earth and imparted to us the heavenly life without leading us up to heaven, but by bending heaven to us in bringing it down. . . .
> This way the Lord traced by coming to us, this gate He opened by entering into the world. When He returned to the Father He suffered it not to be closed, but from Him He comes through it to sojourn among men.[33]

Liturgical mysticism is this gate, still swinging on its hinges after all these centuries, allowing traffic through it. Christ descends,

---

[32] Benedict XVI, *Jesus of Nazareth: Holy Week* (San Francisco: Ignatius Press, 2011), 82–83.
[33] Nicholas Cabasilas, *The Life in Christ* (Crestwood, NY: St. Vladimir's Seminary Press, 1974), 50–51.

and liturgy is established; Christ ascends, and a liturgical gateway is created. By his kenosis Christ opens the gate, and leaves it open! Our liturgical mysticism consists of ascending through the gate that Christ opened whereat the Trinity invites our synergistic ascent into deification.

Christ's ascension causes the Holy Spirit's descension. The synergy of these two persons of the Trinity is a model of the harmony between liturgy and mysticism. Irenaeus spoke of the Son and the Spirit being the two hands of the Father, by which he accomplishes his will. Once upon a time they worked in clay to make Adam and to bring Eve forth from him; now they work on the flesh of our hearts to bring forth the New Eve from the side of the crucified Adam. Divo Barsotti picks up the image:

> So, we have put ourselves in the hands of the Word and in the hands of the Holy Spirit, so that He can create us once more and take us up to the Father. What does this all mean? It means that, for us, to live is to give ourselves to Christ, to surrender ourselves to the Holy Spirit. Or rather, to surrender ourselves to the Holy Spirit so that the Holy Spirit can renew in us the mystery of the life of Christ. So that in us it can continue and prolong the mystery of this divine obedience which took Him to the Cross and from the Cross to Heaven. And so that, through the cross, it can take us too in a glorious ascension to the bosom of God.[34]

We prolong the mystery; we live from mystery to mystery; the image of God is quickened into the likeness of God. The posture we should have on this pathway is described by Paul as straining forward, though we do not own it yet. "Brethren, I do not consider that I have made it my own; but one thing I do, forgetting what lies behind and straining forward to what lies ahead, I press on toward the goal for the prize of the upward call of God in Christ Jesus" (Phil 3:13–14). Gregory of Nyssa uses this passage to describe *epectasis* (the tension or expansion of things). "Even after listening in secret to the mysteries of heaven, Paul does not let the graces he has obtained become the limit of his desire, but he continues to go on and on, never ceasing

---

[34] Divo Barsotti, *Suspended Between Two Abysses: Meditations on Freedom* (n.p.: Chorabooks, 2016), e-book.

his ascent. Thus he teaches us. . . . [That] the graces that we receive at every point are indeed great, but the path that lies beyond our immediate grasp is infinite."[35]

---

[35] Gregory of Nyssa, *Commentary on the Canticle*, quoted in Jean Daniélou's introduction to *From Glory to Glory: Texts from Gregory of Nyssa's Mystical Writings* (Crestwood, NY: St. Vladimir's Seminary Press, 1979), 58.

CHAPTER 7

COMING HOME

(TWENTY YEARS AGO I concocted an introduction for a paper that I was going to present at a conference, but I got cold feet. I was new, I wanted to be taken seriously, I was trying to establish a reputation. Now that I am old, and I take academics more light-heartedly, and my reputation is beyond retrieval, I return to that introduction because it contained an image perfectly suitable for our final topic. It went as follows.)

I have never had the chance to prove it, lacking a grant for a funded study of my hunch, but I have long harbored the suspicion that other co-workers in the guild of Academics also share my satisfying and idle habit of delivering lectures to imaginary audiences. Some of my best orations take place in the shower each morning, my most profound discourses sitting at a red light, and some of the best lectures no one has ever heard have been delivered walking the four blocks to my office with animated countenance and gesticulating hands. Now, I've always thought it a shame that these soliloquies go unnoticed. If a saint's good deeds do not go unnoticed, and a monk's prayers do not go unnoticed, why should a theologian's thoughts go unnoticed? So I like to imagine that in such circumstances I am lecturing to the angels. They are always courteous and polite, but they are also amused and perplexed by my imagination, because the thoughts of angels are not like the thoughts of men. St. Dionysius tells us that the angels "do not draw together their knowledge of God from fragments nor from bouts of perception,"[1] while I do. Yet, Dionysius does also admit that human "sense perceptions also can properly be described as echoes of wisdom,"[2] so I sometimes further imagine God clapping one of the angels jocularly on its ethereal back (thereby answering the old Zen question about the sound of one hand clapping) and exclaiming, "There! Now *that's* what you could do if you had a body, because corporeal creatures have sensations, and sensations create images, and images are the stuff of imagination." This, by the way, is why I think that only angels should strive to do ideal liturgies and we humans should content ourselves with sensible ones.

On one of these short, four block lecture tours, I had an imaginative thought (i.e., a thought rooted in a sense perception) which clarified for me something about liturgy, but the angels could not comprehend it due to their incorporeality. So I promised myself that if I ever had the opportunity to address an august and actual audience of embodied intelligences, I would finish making application of this intuition. The thought was this: *You can't taste your tongue.*

(At this point, I had planned to try and rescue my introduction with a bit of academic sleight-of-hand. This palatable profundity could be used to illustrate the self-reflexive bipolarity which Karl Rahner says is the ground of human transcendental experience. "In knowledge, not only is something known, but the subject's knowing is always co-known."[3] Or we might use it to illustrate the tacit dimension of knowledge in Michael Polanyi's epistemology[4] wherein the object we are knowing is called the distal term, and the many perceptions by which we know it is the proximal term, and he theorizes that we can only know the distal if we do not attend to the proximal. But I shall instead use this insight to make a point about liturgy.)

You can't taste your tongue. Why not? Because the tongue is the organ by which you taste. Likewise, you can't celebrate the liturgy. Why not? Because the liturgy is the organ by which you celebrate . . . what? What does the Church taste in her liturgy? Not herself, I hope.

[1] Dionysius, *The Divine Names*, in *Pseudo-Dionysius: The Complete Works* (New York: Paulist Press, 1987), 106.
[2] Dionysius, *The Divine Names*, 107.
[3] Karl Rahner, *Foundations of Christian Faith* (New York: Seabury Press, 1978), 18.
[4] See part two of *Personal Knowledge: Towards a Post-Critical Philosophy* (Chicago: University of Chicago Press, 1974); *The Tacit Dimension* (New York: Doubleday, 1966); and part three of *Knowing and Being* (Chicago: University of Chicago Press, 1969).

Narcissus was attracted to a pool where he saw his own reflection in the water and fell in love with it; I hope we are not attracted to a liturgy where we see our own reflection in the rite and fall in love with it. Holmer was correct when he said liturgy is not an expression of how people see things; rather it should propose, instead, how God sees all people. We should be celebrating something *in* liturgy, *through* liturgy, *by means of* liturgy, but what is it?

I suggest that we taste the eschaton. Liturgy is a foretaste of the eschaton. The liturgy doesn't exist to be celebrated, the liturgy exists to celebrate, sacramentally, the perpetual presence of the incarnate one who, by unifying the infinite with the finite in his own hypostatic union, makes possible the deification of those with whom this same form of life is shared by grace. In other words, liturgical mysticism.

Eucharistic, liturgical mysticism has an eschatological flavor because it opens our souls on the side of heaven; because what is to come, already is; because "through love, the future is for us already present";[5] because we give our praise in the company of Mary and the saints and the hosts of heaven; because it is the sacrament of love, and God's love is omnipresent and never ending; because the chalice contains the blood of an eternal covenant; because it concerns the single created thing to which there is no end (viz., our souls); because the one who "pitched his tent among us" has now passed through the more perfect tent not made with human hands (John 1:14; Heb 9:11) to continue his role of High Priest; because his resurrection opened once and for all the holy places of God; because like the prodigal son we have been reclothed after our disrobing; because distractions of the world wane as love for God waxes; because the mercy seat of God, once protected in the tabernacle by two cherubim, is now the altar where Christ is enthroned before us; because this is the vestibule of the heavenly mansions about which Jesus spoke; because we bilocate in the Eucharist, standing simultaneously before the earthly altar and the heavenly throne, the earthly ambo and the Lamb as he opens the sealed scrolls.

This eschatology can be tasted in various formulas in the Mass. Here is a cursory list. We beg almighty God to have mercy on us and forgive us our sins in order to bring us to everlasting life; the one who took away the sins of the world and receives our prayer is seated at the right hand of the Father; we beg him to make of us an eternal offering

---

5   Clement of Alexandria, *The Stromata* (n.p.: Aeterna Press, 2016), 337.

to the Father so that we may obtain an inheritance with the elect, Mary, the apostles, the martyrs, the saints; the fruit of the earth and work of human hands becomes for us the bread of life; if the Lord graciously accepts this oblation of our service, and orders our days in his peace, then he will command that we be delivered from eternal damnation and counted among the flock that he has chosen; our gifts are borne by the hands of his holy angel to his altar on high in the sight of his divine majesty. The General Instruction of the Roman Missal also contains various eschatological references. Here is another cursory list. We are instructed that in the acclamation the whole congregation joins with the heavenly powers;[6] that the anamnesis not only fulfills Christ's command but recalls "especially his blessed Passion, glorious Resurrection, and Ascension into heaven";[7] that the intercessions express the fact "the Eucharist is celebrated in communion with the whole Church, of both heaven and of earth";[8] that the sacred building itself, and those things required for divine worship, "should be truly worthy and beautiful and be signs and symbols of heavenly realities."[9]

But proof-texting passages from the Mass is the easy way out, and I would rather not take it. We have a hard paradox to deal with: the Kingdom of God has been established, but it is still history's goal; the Kingdom of God has arrived, but it is still coming; the Kingdom of God is already available, but we still wait for it. Liturgical theology is the enterprise of grasping this fact spiritually, personally, theologically, mystically. Such is Alexander Schmemann's understanding, summarized here in a lengthy quote from his *Journals*:

> Some affirm that only in history, only serving history and its meaning, can man find meaning in his own life. Others, with as much passion, affirm that only in being liberated from history can one find this meaning. The Christians have accepted this "either-or" and submitted themselves to it. This is the tragedy of contemporary Christianity—tragedy because

6 *General Instruction of the Roman Missal*, ch. 2 (Washington, DC: United States Conferences of Catholic Bishops, 2011), §79.b, http://www.usccb.org/prayer-and-worship/the-mass/general-instruction-of-the-roman-missal/girm-chapter-2.cfm.
7 *General Instruction of the Roman Missal*, ch. 2, §79.e.
8 *General Instruction of the Roman Missal*, ch. 2, §79.g.
9 *General Instruction of the Roman Missal*, ch. 5 (Washington, DC: United States Conferences of Catholic Bishops, 2011), §288, http://www.usccb.org/prayer-and-worship/the-mass/general-instruction-of-the-roman-missal/girm-chapter-5.cfm.

ultimately the whole novelty of Christianity consisted (consists) in destroying this choice, this polarization. *This* is the essence of Christianity as Eschatology. The Kingdom of God is the goal of history, and the Kingdom of God is already now *among us, within us.* Christianity is a unique historical event, and Christianity is the presence of that event as the completion of all events and of history itself. . . .

Here is, for me, *the whole meaning of liturgical theology.* The Liturgy: the joining, revelation, actualization of the historicity of Christianity (remembrance) and of its transcendence over that historicity. . . .

Hence, the link of the Church with the world, the Church *for the world,* but as its beginning and its end, as the affirmation that the world is *for the Church,* since the Church is the presence of the kingdom of God.

Here is the eternal antinomy of Christianity and the essence of all contemporary discussions about Christianity. The task of theology is to be faithful to the antinomy, which disappears in the experience of the Church as *pascha:* a *continuous* (not only historical) passage of the world to the Kingdom. All the time one must leave the world and all the time one must remain it.[10]

The antinomy disappears in the Eucharistic event because in the Eucharist the Church actually experiences herself as the passage of the world to the Kingdom. This is not tasting herself; this is not narcissistically feasting on the organization; this is primary theology experiencing the Church's very being. Ontologically, the Church is the world passing into the Kingdom, which is why the liturgy done by that Church is the ontological condition for theology. The antinomy disappears in the Eucharistic event but remains in our thinking, because if the eschatological tension is ever relaxed, like a tightrope walker's cable being loosened, then the faith-walker grows unsteady and falls either into a passivity that waits for some futuristic utopia, or into an activism that wants to make life better before we die. Neither is Christianity's true calling, because the Church is for the world, and the world is for the Church.

---

[10] Alexander Schmemann, *The Journals of Father Alexander Schmemann* (Crestwood, NY: St. Vladimir's Seminary Press, 2002), 234. Emphasis in original.

This suggests that eschatology does not actually operate in ignorance of the world, as it is so often presented. Rather, eschatology recasts our experience and understanding of the world. To appreciate that, notice the different meanings or uses of "world" as a concept. First, it can mean things as they are, the cosmos, God's good gift, the first chapter of Genesis. Second, it can mean an internal subjective state, how we internalize reality, our world-view, adults and children occupy different worlds. Third, it can mean the fallen world, a sinful state, the third chapter of Genesis, which is why the same gospel that says God so loved the world that he gave his only Son for it (John 3:16) also says that Jesus's disciples do not belong to the world (John 17:16), that the world hates them (John 15:19) and they must hate their life in this world (John 12:23), that they long for the judgment of this world at which time the spirit that rules this world will be driven out (John 12:30). Theologians sometimes stop here, satisfied with these three definitions, but if they do, they may be tempted toward a reduction that results in moral dualism: something good has become something bad, and must be flipped back again. And since this repair will not happen until the eschaton, Christians in the meantime needn't be much interested in this present damaged and defective world, and liturgy is where they go to "wait it out." If the Eucharist is irrelevant to the world, and the world is irrelevant to the Eucharist, then Schmemann's antinomy has failed.

I propose there is a fourth meaning of "world," and faithfulness to the antinomy of eschatology in the Eucharist will reveal it. This fourth definition understands the world as incomplete, unfinished, something still partial and waiting to be filled full. World number four is the sphere of becoming: it is potentiality awaiting actuality, the place of voyage from *ex nihilo* to a depth of ontology not yet acquired. Liturgical mystery moves the world toward its telos. In other words, eschatology is not the study of annihilation, it is the study of consummation. The eschaton is the world completed, perfected, concluded; it is the world beautified, beatified, splendored; it is the world verified, substantiated, fulfilled. The presence of eschaton is the fullness of time, not the voiding of time (Gal 4:4), and this is precisely what we celebrate Eucharistically. You can't taste the liturgy because you aren't supposed to be sucking on the liturgy. The Eucharist is a foretaste of the goodness of God as He consummates his creation in truth and beauty. Mystically taste and see the Kingdom of God, which is a new heaven and a new earth, a new Jerusalem, a new humanity whose progenitor is Jesus.

We are still standing in the flow of history, but the thing toward which history runs already stands within the flow, beside us, for our tasting and seeing—that is Schmemann's point. That is his definition of a liturgical theology that lives in and thinks from the antinomy of a history that has its endpoint already present within it, even as it still awaits fulfillment. It is a difficult question: How can we possibly see the risen and ascended Christ while we are still buried neck deep in the transitory sands of time? The answer is given by the priest when he simply lifts up Jesus and bids us to *"Behold* the Lamb of God, *behold* him who takes away the sins of the world." The telos of history is here: look at him! Happy are those who espy him and mystically taste his love. The one who has gone ahead is still present, the triumphant one still marches with his Church militant, the one awaiting us accompanies us on our pilgrimage to the many rooms he has prepared for us in his Father's house. The task of theology is to be faithful to the antinomy, but the antinomy disappears in the experience of the Church as *pascha,* which is an experience of the continuous passage of the world to the Kingdom. That is why liturgy's *theologia prima* is the source-foundation of theology: the eschatological linkage of life and the Kingdom is what liturgical theology expresses, and liturgical mysticism experiences.

There are sins of the world that our Lord Jesus, only Begotten Son, Lamb of God, Son of the Father, came to take away. But those sins are not, as the dualists thought, sins of being material. Speaking of the world as "fallen" almost inevitably leads us to imagine some sort of cascade from spirit into matter, in the dualist sense of the Manichees, Docetists, Albigensians, and even a low-grade fever of spiritualism still sported today by those who prefer to be "spiritual instead of religious." All of these operate with an inaccurate diagnosis of our human condition. Augustine thought his way out of them by realizing that evil is a privation, and the tradition has developed the understanding that sin is a privation, a lack, leading me to suggest that sin is not *falling from,* it is *falling short.* Adam and Eve were *short-sighted* when they forfeited their liturgical career as cosmic priests; they *shortchanged* God, defrauding him of the latria rightfully his; ontology was *cut short,* stunted, and aborted when the world was only seen for selfish utility and its sacramental character obscured. Our problem is not that we are made of matter, our problem is that we sinners do not use matter for the twofold end for which it was created: sacramental theophany by God and sacrificial oblation by man. Correcting the diagnosis of our pathology would correct our understanding of soteriology. Redemption does not consist of being temporarily evacuated on a Sunday morning from a material world into a spiritual haze, it consists of rectifying the proper use of matter (asceticism). It is right and just to lift up our hearts and give thanks to the Lord our God with bodies and oblations. The range of liturgical piety is our whole life long, as we strive to do the world the way it was meant to be done. The Eucharist is the world completed, not escaped, which can only be accomplished by those who have had their cosmic priesthood rectified by baptism so that they can bring the cosmos before God in anamnetic imitation of Christ's perfect sacrifice.

One of the mysteries of iniquity is how a good world can be the cause of worldliness. How can the world that God concluded, after careful inspection, to be "very good" (Gen 1:31) be an occasion for sin? Perhaps a definition of worldliness is in order. Worldliness is using the world without reference to God. Worldliness is the absence of faith wherein faith is recognition of God in the world. We may take the world; God intended it so; he gave it to us to lead us to himself. C. S. Lewis says the beauties of this world are only images of what we really desire.

> They are only the scent of a flower we have not found, the echo of a tune we have not heard, news from a country we have never yet visited. Do you think I am trying to weave a spell? Perhaps I am; but remember your fairy tales. Spells are used for breaking enchantments as well as for inducing them. And you and I have need of the strongest spell that can be found to wake us from the evil enchantment of worldliness which has been laid upon us for nearly a hundred years. Almost our whole education has been directed to silencing this shy, persistent, inner voice; almost all our modern philosophies have been devised to convince us that the good of man is to be found on this earth.[11]

But worldliness is the disruption of this primordial sacramentality. Worldliness is the sinfully enchanted belief that our good is to be found only, finally, primarily, exclusively on this earth. Worldliness

---

[11] C. S. Lewis, "The Weight of Glory," in *The Weight of Glory and Other Essays* (San Francisco: HarperSanFrancisco, 2007), 6–7.

erases the divine horizon, takes time and matter and history and objects in themselves, for ourselves, without reference to God. Worldliness is treating the passing as permanent, the shadow as body, the ephemeral as eternal, the pathway as home. What we require is a spell-breaking liturgical mysticism that illuminates the truth about the world.

Liquid is matter lacking fixed shape, and we call such a condition "watery"; wind is moving air that is not stable, and we call such a condition "windy"; world refers to passing time that is not permanent, and we call such a condition "worldly." It is not evil to be impermanent, but it is evil to understand the world that will pass away as our permanent home. Lallemant says, "[I]f we love the esteem and applause of the world, we are fools; we feed ourselves with wind."[12] Libermann gives a stinging comparison: "With regard to the esteem and affection of men, it is not worth-while taking them seriously. Let us suppose that I come from a neighbor's house. His little dog has shown me great affection and made very much of me. I esteem myself neither the better nor the happier for it. The same applies when people show this esteem for you."[13]

Now, eschatology is the opposite of worldliness. Worldliness stops short, while eschatology follows the teleological trajectory to the ultimate end. Worldliness affixes our attention on the image instead of on its prototype, while eschatology contemplates the archetype in the created ectype. To look at our life in a worldly manner is to lower our gaze from the eternal to the immediate, from the horizon to the abridged, from the enduring to the transitory, from the certain to the contingent, from providence to chance, from the necessary to the superfluous. To look at our life in the world in a liturgical manner is to understand it to be not complete in itself but to be a pathway to God.

This fact has been emphasized by all Christian spiritual writers, but often misunderstood by modern readers. That is, Christian spiritual writers have been misunderstood to be rejecting the world as evil, when they were actually tightening the antinomy: all the time you remain in the world you must be leaving it. They did so because they

---

[12] Lallemant, *The Spiritual Doctrine of Father Louis Lallemant of the Company of Jesus: Preceded by Some Account of His Life* (New York: Sadlier, 1885), 72.

[13] Francis Libermann, *The Spiritual Letters of the Venerable Francis Libermann*, vol. 4, "Letters to Clergy and Religious," in Duquesne Studies, Spiritan Series 8, ed. Walter Van De Putte (Pittsburgh: Duquesne University Press, 1964), 39.

tasted the resolution of the antinomy in the Eucharistic *pascha*. The world is temporal, temporary, transitory—that is its natural condition as a finite creation—and spiritual writers have tried to awaken us whenever we misconstrue the transient as sufficient. We can find this in any spiritual writing we look at, and I share only the most recent sample I have read. It comes from the story of *Barlaam and Josaphat*.[14] In it, the master opens his disciple's eyes by saying,

> Following the teachings of these Blessed Saints, we utterly renounce these corruptible and perishable things of life where there may be found nothing stable or constant or that continues in one state; . . . for they are slighter than dreams in a shadow or the breeze that blows the air. Small and short-lived is their charm.[15]

The disciple is persuaded, so he responds,

> When I perceived, with the unerring eyes of my mind, how all human life is wasted in these things that come and go; when I saw that no man has anything that is stable and steadfast, neither the rich in his wealth, nor the mighty in his strength, nor the wise in his wisdom, nor the prosperous in his prosperity . . . nor any man in any of those things that men on earth commend; then, I say, I understood that all such things are vanity. . . . [E]ven as the past is all buried in oblivion, be it past glory, or past kingship, or the splendor of rank, or amplitude of power, or arrogance of tyranny, or anything else like them, so also present things will vanish in the darkness of the days to come.[16]

The fruit of mystical contemplation gives us a distaste for the passing world, but only because we see its vainglory, not because of some dualist reasoning that the material world is evil. No prosperity, no wisdom, no splendor of rank is meant to last on its own legs, and to invest

---

[14] Once attributed to John of Damascus but now thought to derive from a Georgian monk of the eleventh century.
[15] Saint John Damascene, *The Precious Pearl: The Lives of Saints Barlaam and Ioasaph* (Belmont, MA: Institute for Byzantine and Modern Greek Studies, 1997), 154.
[16] Damascene, *The Precious Pearl*, 168.

ourselves in them is vanity. Our experiences in this world are instead opportunities to condition our soul for its journey to the Eternal One, who does live forever. Thus, John Chrysostom confides,

> Everyone of you can ascend the seraphic heights, if only you want to do so. Only recall and gather in your memory all the most beautiful things that you have seen on earth and which have delighted you, and reflect that all these things were so lovely only because they were a reflection of the great heavenly beauty, only the gleaming hem of the mere mantle of God, and of itself your soul will be transported to the Bosom and Source of eternal beauty and will sing the song of triumph, casting itself down with the Seraphim before the eternal throne of the Most High.[17]

The soul grieves at the shortcomings of the praise it can currently give. What it wants is to ascend to new heights where it can give adequate glory to God. The key to eschatology is liturgical latria.

We suffer a sickness unto death by taking the world without reference to God, and the cure for our condition is to finally take the world *with* reference to God, which is the eschatological therapy we undergo at Eucharist. Through God's goodness we have received the bread we offer him, fruit of the earth and work of human hands, which will become for us the bread of life, a medicament that will promote recovery from our injury and healing of our disease. Our cure is to see all human things—be it glory, or rank, or power, or esteem—in their right light. We may use the world, but we must use it on the correct terms, for its correct end, and we learn those terms and end when we stand before the Unchangeable One in formal latria, bringing him our ever-changing lives in oblation. The Eucharist does not abandon this world, it brings this world to the throne of God to serve the Kingdom.

Eschatology has to do with end things (i.e., the condition of things in their final state). Human beings are in their end state when they celebrate the Mass because offering our peaceful oblation is the final state for which God created us. In the Orthodox liturgy of St. John Chrysostom, the deacon cries out, "Let us stand aright! Let us

---

[17] John Chrysostom, quoted in Nikolai Gogol, *Meditations on the Divine Liturgy* (Jordanville, NY: Holy Trinity Monastery, 1985), 40.

stand with fear! Let us attend! That we may offer the Holy Oblation in peace." We are in our end state when we offer our hearts in sacrifice and enjoy the abiding presence of God. That is what we taste in liturgy (not our own tongue). Saying liturgy is symbolic is an eschatologically ontological statement. It reveals the x-ray quality of sacramental liturgy that sees through the temporal rite to the eternal eschaton. In fact, suggests Metropolitan Hierotheos, there are two liturgies going on for the hesychastic mystic who has recovered his noetic faculty.

> Something happens that seems strange to most people, but is natural for those who consciously practice hesychia. Although they are present at the Divine Eucharist and are aware through their senses and their reason of everything that is going on, they are listening at the same time to the noetic faculty in the heart, where the Holy Spirit praises without ceasing: "Lord Jesus Christ, Son of God, have mercy on me." In other words, there are two liturgies. One is the external Liturgy of the Divine Eucharist, where the bread and wine are changed into the Body and Blood of Christ in the Holy Spirit. The other is the inner liturgy or eucharist, where they experience uncreated worship and the spiritual priest of divine grace celebrates. There is no break between the two liturgies; both are accomplished with full awareness. The Holy Spirit changes the bread and wine into Christ's Body and Blood, and the same Holy Spirit activates noetic prayer on the altar of the heart.[18]

The mystics are sharp-eyed at this and help teach the rest of us. The symbols of liturgy are not designed to create a nostalgia for Galilee, they are designed to make a statement about the ontological truth of a thing's proper end. That is why we use we use matter in liturgy, explains Paul Evdokimov. "The final destiny of water is to participate in the mystery of the Epiphany; of wood, to become a cross; of the earth, to receive the body of the Lord during his rest on the Sabbath. . . . Olive oil and water attain their fullness as conductor elements for grace on regenerated man. Wheat and wine achieve their ultimate *raison*

---

[18] Metropolitan Hierotheos, *Hesychia and Theology: The Context for Man's Healing in the Orthodox Church* (Levadia, Greece: Birth of the Theotokos Monastery, 2007), 438.

d'etre in the eucharistic chalice."[19] This is a dimension of transubstantiation, though often overlooked, claims Benedict XVI. "[The Eucharist] is the real 'action' for which all of creation is in expectation. The elements of the earth are transubstantiated, pulled, so to speak, from their creaturely anchorage, grasped at the deepest ground of their being, and changed into the Body and Blood of the Lord. The New Heaven and the New Earth are anticipated."[20] Transubstantiation detects the eschatological work going on beneath liturgical symbols to reveal the sacramental purpose of creation, even as it sacramentally effects the end of man, which is communion with God.

Modern folk sniffingly dismiss certain elements of liturgical commentaries as allegorical, but I think those liturgical commentators never intended to treat the Eucharist as simply an allegorical *tableau vivant* of heaven; instead they intended us to really detect the presence of the heavenly liturgy in ours. That is why the commentators picture heaven happening in the liturgy's symbolic acts. When the commentators said the deacons waving fans were like the angels brandishing their wings in heaven, it was because they knew that angels were really tending this altar, too. In his commentary on the Divine Liturgy, Nikolai Gogol says that when the Holy Doors are opened, it is "as though they were the gates of heaven itself, and before the eyes of the whole congregation stands the resplendent altar as the dwelling of God's glory and the supreme seat of learning from which the knowledge of the truth goes out to us and eternal life is proclaimed."[21] Schmemann makes a similar point in his own description of the entrance rite.

> It has been given all possible symbolic explanations, but it is not a "symbol." It is the very movement of the Church as *passage* from the old into the new, from "this world" into the "world to come" and, as such, it is the essential movement of the liturgical "journey." In "this world" there is no altar and the temple has been destroyed. For the only altar is Christ Himself, His humanity which He has assumed and deified

---

[19] Paul Evdokimov, *The Art of the Icon: A Theology of Beauty* (Redondo Beach, CA: Oakwood, 1990), 117–118.

[20] Joseph Ratzinger, *The Spirit of the Liturgy* (San Francisco: Ignatius Press, 2000), 173.

[21] Nikolai Gogol, *Meditations on the Divine*, 22.

and made the temple of God, the altar of His presence. And Christ ascended into heaven. The altar thus is the sign that in Christ we have been given access to heaven, that the Church is the "passage" to heaven, the entrance into the heavenly sanctuary. . . . It is not "grace" that comes down; it is the Church that enters into "grace," and grace means the new being, the Kingdom, the world to come.[22]

What sets the tone in these liturgical commentaries is not an overactive allegorical imagination, but an eschatological perceptiveness. The eschaton is actually tasted in these symbols. The same instinct populates the Church with statues and icons of saints because Christians know we are now joined by the citizens of heaven at our earthly liturgy, as one day we will join them at their heavenly liturgy. The liturgies are banded together. The General Instruction of the Roman Missal says, "In the earthly Liturgy, the Church participates, by a foretaste, in that heavenly Liturgy which is celebrated in the holy city of Jerusalem, toward which she journeys as a pilgrim."[23] The liturgical lodestone always points home. It provides a link, says Louis Bouyer.

The sacramental world is essentially a link between two other worlds, the world of eternity, in which the risen Christ lives, and the world of today, in which we have to live and achieve in ourselves the life of the risen. To be still more precise, the sacramental world is the link between the achievement of the divine life in an ordinary human existence exemplified by the historical life of Jesus, and the achievement of the same life in our own existence.[24]

Mysticism ascends from this world to a new eon, and the sacramental world is the link between them.

The sacramental world being described here has its origin in baptism. Perhaps we need a more vigorous view of baptism if we are to appreciate the links between divine life and our human existence

[22] Alexander Schmemann, *For the Life of the World* (Crestwood, NY: St. Vladimir's Seminary Press, 1973), 31.
[23] *General Instruction of the Roman Missal*, ch. 5, §318.
[24] Louis Bouyer, *Christian Initiation* (New York: McMillan, 1960), 116.

being described. What if we pictured baptism not as a stagnant pond, but as a waterfall that curtains one world from another? Catechumens should feel its full crashing force when they pass through the wall of water to discover a valley on its other side containing the trailhead to paradise. They arrive at the Church, which houses a table placed at the beginning of the end of the world. It is akin to the table Lewis describes in one of the books in the *Chronicles of Narnia*. When Lucy asks why it is called Aslan's table, she is told, "It is set here by his bidding . . . for those who come so far. Some call this island the World's End, for though you can sail further, this is the beginning of the end."[25] The Sunday morning liturgy is not the end, for we can sail further, but it is the beginning of the end. You can see the eschaton from the Eucharistic altar. Set upon that table in Narnia is a feast for nourishment and the knife that killed Aslan long ago, kept in honor while the world lasts; set upon the altar in our world is viaticum for pilgrimage and the cross that killed our Lord long ago, kept here in his honor so that whenever "we eat this Bread and drink this Cup, we proclaim your Death, O Lord, until you come again."

The catechumen has been prepared for this feast for three long years, or more, and in the waterfall has received three virtues to equip him for the eating and the journey. Francis de Sales excellently organizes those theological virtues around a desire, a desire we can properly recognize as eschatological. We will never be satiated by liturgy, because what we taste here is designed to awaken *more* hunger, a sort of hungry desire that de Sales describes as an interweaving of faith, hope, and love circulating round our sovereign good. The more we hope for what we believe, the more we love what we believe. Love turns its desire into hope, and hope is expectant love.

> As soon as faith has shown me my sovereign good, I have loved it; and because it was absent I have desired it, and having understood that it would bestow itself upon me, I have loved and desired it yet more ardently. . . . Now by this progress love has turned its desire into hope, seeking and expectation, so that hope is an expectant and aspiring love; and because the sovereign good which hope expects is God, and because also she expects it from God himself, to whom and

---

[25] C. S. Lewis, *The Voyage of the Dawn Treader*, in *The Chronicles of Narnia* (New York: HarperCollins, 2001), 518.

by whom she hopes and aspires, this holy virtue of hope, abutting everywhere on God, is by consequence a divine or theological virtue.[26]

We are sacramentally wed to God, but we are waiting for the eschatological wedding night when we will consummate our nuptials. Therefore we actually hope that one day the sacrament will come to an end! De Sales again:

> O God! What sweetness shall it be for man's understanding to be united for ever to its sovereign object, receiving not its representation but its presence, not the picture or species, but the very essence of its divine truth and majesty. . . . Infinite bliss, Theotimus, and one which has not been promised only, but of which we have a pledge in the Blessed Sacrament, that perpetual feast of Divine Grace. For in it we receive the blood of Our Saviour in his flesh, and his flesh in his blood . . . that we may know that so he will apply unto us his divine essence in the eternal feast of his glory. True it is, this favor is done unto us here really but covertly, under sacramental species and appearances, whereas in heaven, the Divinity will give himself openly, and we shall see him face to face as he is.[27]

It is a strange gastronomy. The Eucharist increases our hunger, it does not satisfy it; the Eucharist amplifies our thirst, it does not satiate it. Our taste for the eschaton has been dulled under the spell a worldly world has cast, but Eucharistic eating has the reverse effect, and we get hungrier as we eat. This is the key to liturgical mysticism.

Doing the world as it is meant to be done is hungry work. Every Eucharist—not just the last one—is a viaticum, a provision for a continual journey. While the Church waits for Christ to come and clear his threshing-floor (Matt 3), she is in the position of the widow of Zarephath whom Elijah asks for a crust of bread. There is only a handful of flour in her jar, and a little oil, and when she, the Church, has prepared something for her children, she expects her resources to be exhausted, and to die. But Elijah, the prophet of the Messiah, the one who has a plate setting at every Passover Seder, the one who did

---

[26] Francis de Sales, *Treatise on the Love of God* (Blacksburg, VA: Wilder, 2011), 108.

[27] De Sales, *Treatise on the Love of God*, 142.

not die and kept an appointment with Jesus on Mount Tabor, says to her, the Church, "Do not be afraid. The jar of flour shall not go empty; you will be able to bake bread for the sacrament of love for as long as history lasts." The liturgical mystic is not afraid.

Why are we leaving the world? De Sales answers it is because "the amorous soul, [perceives] that she cannot satiate the desire she has to praise our well-beloved while she lives in this world."[28] We are attracted by the lure of a latria that is more satisfying than any dulia we can give here, now. We have a foretaste of that latria when we receive our participatory share of Jesus's piety. Every Eucharist is a parousia, an arrival, a coming, an advent, the visit of a king, a royal visit, which helps us realize, according to Benedict XVI, "that whereas in the Liturgy the Church appears to be engaged in self-contemplation, in reality she enters into the heart of the world, and works actively for the latter's liberating transformation. . . . The trumpet of the Word is already summoning us, and yet it is still to be sounded. Every Eucharist is Parousia, the Lord's coming, and yet the Eucharist is even more truly the tensed yearning that he would reveal his hidden Glory."[29] The seven trumpets in the Book of Revelation are not sounding retreat. Isaiah says that on the mountain God will destroy the veil that veils all peoples, destroying death forever, so the people of faith are encamped on the foothills of this mountain as they wait to ascend it. Just so, the Eucharistic viaticum we receive gives us fortitude for the upcoming climb.

The world in rebellion (I'm speaking of our hearts) will not easily enter into that ascent. The thin air of that mystical altitude will threaten the heavy fog of worldliness we are accustomed to breathing. Eschatology has a cutting edge to it, which is why we tend to avoid it. That is why theologians tend to house eschatology in their speculative theology instead of in practical theology: liturgical asceticism is necessary for mystical ascent, and we fear it. A new beginning requires an end, and we fear endings, warns Louis Bouyer.

> Christianity asserts quite unambiguously that neither the individual nor the collective salvation of humanity is possible either on earth or in any possible prolongation of the present

---

[28] De Sales, *Treatise on the Love of God,* 190.

[29] Joseph Ratzinger, *Eschatology: Death and Eternal Life* (Washington, DC: Catholic University of America Press, 1988), 208.

state of affairs. Christianity is, as they say, eschatological. That is, it rests on a belief in the end of time. . . . An anticipation of this golden age is certainly possible for each individual. But this anticipation itself can only come here after: after our individual death, when, if we have been faithful to the risen Christ on earth, he will give us a foretaste of universal resurrection.[30]

Schmemann said that all the time we must be leaving this world while all the time remaining in it, and now we see the reason for this antinomy: the Christian must follow his Lord, and our Lord both entered the world and left it. We must first follow Jesus's path in. The Church's liturgical mimesis of his life means that we follow his footprints to Zacchaeus's house, to the well in Samaria, to the table of Matthew the tax collector, to the demon-possessed and the diseased. Then we must follow Jesus's footprints out. The Church's liturgical mimesis of his life means we follow an exit path, but it is a pathway marked with crosses. Our path to glory takes us on a bridge built over the center axis of the world, right over the skull and bones of Adam under the cross (as pictured in icons), upon which we struggle with the death of our self-love. Francis Libermann sees eternal life served up at Eucharist as "the germ of our future resurrection. . . . Our union must begin in this world and it ought to keep on increasing until it is finally consummated in heaven. Holy Communion is a heaven for the Christian soul."[31] The Eucharist feeds us on eternal life, which is "life begun in this world which will have no end."[32]

The Eucharist is a foreshadow of the eschaton, and the eschaton is the judgment that will shake the walls of our world. So we should end by saying something about our ending. Bouyer called it a catastrophe, meaning an overturning, a sudden end. Eschatology "asserts that human history must end in a catastrophe, that it will be interrupted by the supremely miraculous event, the return of Christ and the universal judgment and resurrection. After that, but only after that, the salvation of humanity will be possible."[33] But J. R. R. Tolkien clarifies that it will actually be a *eucatastrophe*: a sudden and

---

[30] Bouyer, *Christian Initiation*, 113.
[31] Libermann, *The Spiritual Letters*, 4:50, 52.
[32] Francis Libermann, *Jesus Through Jewish Eyes*, vol. 3 (Dublin: Paraclete Press / Blackrock College, 2005), 80.
[33] Bouyer, *Christian Initiation*, 113.

favorable resolution. "In the 'eucatastrophe' we see in a brief vision that the answer may be greater—it may be a far-off gleam or echo of *evangelium* in the real world."[34] That gleam and echo in what he calls *faerie* accounts for what makes them appeal to our deepest selves. "I was deeply moved and had that peculiar emotion we all have—though not often. It is quite unlike any other sensation. And all of a sudden I realized what it was: the very thing that I have been trying to write about and explain—in that fairy-story essay that I so much wish you had read that I think I shall send it to you. For in it I coined the word 'eucatastrophe': the sudden happy turn in a story which pierces you with a joy that brings tears (which I argued it is the highest function of fairy-stories to produce)."[35] Fairy tales are enjoyed because they have an eschatological scent.

The Eucharist takes measure of the passage of time by placing it against the background of eternity. We should therefore no longer deceive ourselves about what is happening, says Gregory the Great. While we advance, we lose.

> By a very suitable image the time of the flesh is compared to a web. For as the web advances by threads, so this mortal life by the several days; but in proportion as it grows to its bigness, it is advancing to its cutting off. . . . By the same act, by which it augments itself in growth, that is rendered less which remains. Just so with the periods of our life, we as it were rolled up below those that are past, and unwind at top those that are to come, in that the same proportion that the past becomes more, the future have begun to diminish.[36]

And:

> While the step of the traveler too is advancing over the ground in front, what remains of the way is lessening. . . . Whilst the time in our hands passes, the time before us is shortened. And of the whole space of our lives those portions

[34] J. R. R. Tolkien, *On Fairy Stories*, in *Tree and Leaf* (London: HarperCollins, 1988), 71.
[35] J. R. R. Tolkien, *The Letters of J. R. R. Tolkien* (Boston: Houghton Mifflin, 1981), 100.
[36] Gregory the Great, *Moralia of Job*, vol. 1 (n.p.: Ex Fontibus, 2012), 401.

are rendered fewer that are to come, in proportion as those are many in number that have gone by.[37]

This is the way it is in the old eon.

We are in an inferior bargaining position with Saturnus, whose sickle cuts time out from under our feet before our lives can accumulate in any depth. If we were forced to live in his day, Saturday, then the best we could do is eat, drink, and be merry—which is how Gregory the Great describes the witless strategy of worldly persons:

> They place all their hope in transitory things, they aim to have nothing but such objects as pass away. And while they think too much of transitory things, and never look forward to those that shall remain, the eye of their heart is so closed in insensible blindness, that it is never fixed on the interior light. Whence it often happens, that distress already shakes the frame, and approaching death cuts off the power of the breath of life, yet they never cease to mind the things that are of the world. And already the avenger is dragging them to judgment, and yet they themselves, occupied with the concerns of time, in the busy management of them, are only thinking how they may still live on in this world. . . . For by the hardened soul death is still believed to be far off, even when his touch is felt.[38]

But it is possible to surpass Saturday's realm, move beyond the limits and powers of Cronus's shadowland, where he eats his children and swallows up passing generations. Sunday has irrupted. The eighth day has elbowed its way in, giving us a choice between the day of Saturn and the day of the Sun. It is the choice between being a carnal man or a spiritual man, says Gregory.

> Carnal minds only delight in present things, because they never weigh well how transitory the life of the flesh is. For if they regarded the speed of its flight, they would never love it even when it smiled upon them. But Holy Church, in her elect members, daily minds how quick a flight belongs to out-

---

[37] Gregory the Great, *Moralia of Job*, 1:390.
[38] Gregory the Great, *Moralia of Job*, 1:401–402.

ward things, and therefore she sets firm the foot of serious purpose in the interior.[39]

As we stressed earlier, happiness depends upon establishing the right relationship between the outward and inward, what is below and what is above, what we have now and what we will have then, and stabilizing these pairs by liturgical asceticism. Liturgical mysticism distinguishes the pathway from the home, and comes from a labor that merits restful delight. The elect member "reckons the present life to be his road, not his country; a warfare, not the palm of victory."[40] Here is the state of the Church militant, marching through history with an eschatological vantage point gained from the higher ground of standing at the altar of the Lord every eighth day to be fed on the bread of immortality. You can't taste your tongue, but you can taste the eternal with your liturgy. The quick evaporation of all other tastes from the mouth makes clear what we *should* be chewing on.

---

[39] Gregory the Great, *Moralia of Job*, 1:400.
[40] Gregory the Great, *Moralia of Job*, 1:390.

EPILOGUE

WHEN ALEXANDER SCHMEMANN called *leitourgia* the ontological condition for theology, he was not talking about going to a corner of the library shelf to study liturgy. He was talking about ecclesiology.

> The Church is not an institution that keeps certain divinely revealed "doctrines" and "teachings" about this or that event of the past, but the very epiphany of these events themselves. And she can teach about them because, first of all, she knows them; because she is the experience of their reality. Her faith as teaching and theology is rooted in her faith as experience. Her *lex credendi* is revealed in her life.[1]

And from this he concludes that all genuine theology is mystical, not for the reason that it is "at the mercy of individual and irrational 'visions' and 'experiences,' but that it is rooted in, and made indeed *possible*, by the Church's experience of herself as *communion of the Holy Spirit*."[2] Aidan Kavanagh insists that the liturgy does not present mystery from a distance for our consideration. "As Christians have traditionally understood it, their liturgy does not merely approach or reflect upon all this from without, nor does it merely circle this mystery from a distant orbit. Rather, Christians have traditionally

---

[1] Alexander Schmemann, "Liturgy and Theology," in *Liturgy and Tradition*, ed. Thomas Fisch (Crestwood, NY: St. Vladimir's Seminary Press, 1990), 90.

[2] Alexander Schmemann, "Freedom in the Church," in *Church, World, Mission* (Crestwood, NY: Saint Vladimir's Seminary Press, 1979), 188.

understood their liturgical efforts to be somehow enacting the mystery itself, locking together its divine and human agents in a graced commerce."[3] Theology is made possible by the Church's experience in *leitourgia* of the communion of the Holy Spirit, and when the mystic is in communion with the Church, then his or her liturgical theology is by definition mystical.

As I conclude writing, I continue to think about the "content" of *leitourgia* (like reading an ingredients list on the side of a jar), and I find the narration of liturgical theology to be interminable, like the way a relationship with a living human being could have limitless description. Our de-scripting writes down words, but these are words about an existential reality in process. Considering the mystical nature of liturgy has helped reveal this. Gregory's three categories assisted with this dilation because they kept the mystical dimension before our eyes. Liturgy is a visible, outward act, yes; but it is oriented to an inward, invisible *leitourgia* that occurs in our hearts and suffuses our lives. Liturgy is not less than ceremony, but it is certainly more than the ceremony. Latria requires us to go deeper. Liturgy happens on the face of the earth, yes, but in mystical connection with the heavenly liturgy. Liturgy happens now, in chronological, linear time, yes, but because of the presence of the eternal it is also eschatological. In other words, when we step into the visible liturgy of the Church, we should also be stepping into the invisible liturgical mystery within, the heavenly liturgical mystery above, and the eschatological fulfillment of that liturgy to come. When we step into this hour of visible liturgy, the mind descends to the *interior* of the heart, our love ascends to God *above*, and we are *tending* toward our consummation.

Pavel Florensky worried about a propensity in modernity to fragment and isolate. He describes it as "the destruction of form as a real principal."[4] Form is destroyed when one thinks that everything is no more than a collection of separate elements, so the whole is fragmented into parts. To the contrary, Florensky believes, "The whole precedes the parts, and the parts develop out of the whole,"[5] which means that the parts *reveal* the form, they do not produce it. And Florensky proposes an arresting example. "Pushkin's poem *Eugene*

3   Aidan Kavanagh, *On Liturgical Theology* (New York: Pueblo, 1984), 120.
4   Florensky, *At the Crossroads of Science and Mysticism* (Kettering, OH: Semantron Press, an imprint of Angelico Press, 2014), 23. Emphasis added.
5   Florensky, *At the Crossroads*, 24.

Onegin precedes its letters and appears in the case of a certain selection of letters, but not in the case of a random collection of letters."[6] The poem precedes its letters. The letters are selected in service to the poem, which precedes it. Liturgical theology is primary because it precedes *theologia secunda* the way the poem precedes the letters.[7] I think liturgical mysticism can aid us today because it recognizes the formality of liturgy, as Holmer argued. Liturgical theology seeks to know this substance, the form, the latria, the *leitourgia*, which is prior to our performance of liturgy. Secondary theology studies mysteries, but only as fast as our intellect can run; primary theology embraces the mystery, and does so faster than our intellect can run.

Divo Barsotti makes a similar point when he writes, "In theology Christianity finds its doctrine, but in liturgical cult Christianity finds its very self. The Church could never be equated with her theology, but she may be equated with her liturgy, because in cult she finds her doctrine and her life, all her doctrine and all her life."[8]

The sacramental, cultic liturgy brings fire down from heaven, as Elijah did on Mount Carmel, for the purpose of setting our personal, mystical liturgy alight. Christ is the mystery we have been talking about, so when he shares himself, he shares mystery—not as an object of knowledge in the ordinary sense, but as a principle of life which will work in us. So Barsotti adds, "[I]t is in liturgy that Christianity is one grand, divine Mystery, because the Unity of the divine Mystery is not found in a conceptual synthesis executed by man, but truly in an act that is at the same time of man and of God."[9] Liturgy is a free and conscious human act—it must be—but the principal liturgist is the Holy Spirit. The mystical life of believers is their immersion and assimilation into the mystery that Christ accomplished and that we continue to encounter in liturgical cult. The liturgical energy of God invites our synergistic response, yes, but even our ritual liturgy is itself animated by the Holy Spirit who has been placed within us so that

---

[6] Florensky, *At the Crossroads*, 24.

[7] More on this in Fagerberg, "The Liturgy Behind Liturgies: The Church's Metaphysical Form," in *Between Being and Time: From Ontology to Eschatology*, ed. Andrew T. J. Kaethler and Sotiris Mitralexis (New York: Lexington Books / Fortress Academic, 2019), 65–81.

[8] Divo Barsotti, *Il mistero Cristiano nell'anno liturgico* (1951; Cinisello Balsamo, Italy: San Paolo Edizioni, 2006); in English as *The Christian Mystery in the Liturgical Year* (forthcoming). Emphasis added.

[9] Barsotti, *The Christian Mystery*.

we are capable of welcoming Christ when he approaches. Coming to faith requires God to draw out man and woman, and this out-drawing is the mystical dimension to liturgical theology. Theology is union with God; theology is mysticism; the theologia we practice in liturgy is union with God; therefore liturgical theology should reveal liturgy's mystical heart.

At one point, Gregory the Great speaks of Christ as the cornerstone who unites Jew and Gentile, and he offers an interesting definition of a corner. He says, "Where the order is diverted from its right course to go into a different direction, it makes, as it were, a corner."[10] When the course of bricks is diverted from its northward course to begin going eastward, it has turned a corner. Now imagine another kind of corner. The path of our life ought to take a liturgical corner and diverge from the entropic course it is on. However, our life will not escape the disorder of a fallen world by turning a different direction on the same plane: a northward course diverted to an eastward course will still bump into death. No, we need a different plane altogether. Liturgical mysticism takes an *eschatological corner* that turns up toward heaven. Liturgy is the cornerstone on which liturgical theology turns from natural to supernatural, from image of God to likeness of God, from finitude to infinitude, from death to eternal life, from autonomy to theonomy, from the anxiety that Adam and Eve felt when they were hiding to a holy boldness and undaunted audacity before God.

Christ, the rejected stone, has laid himself as an altar in the sanctuary to be that very cornerstone, intersecting the walls of our lives that extend outward and inward, below and above, now and then. In front of his tomb was a stone, but he passed through it, then laid it in his temple as an altar stone, in order that we might pass through that same stone door with him, out of death, and redirect our course toward eternal life. His stone door was marked with the blood of a new Passover Lamb on its lintel and post, but this time it did not simply frighten off death, as did the typological sacramental blood in Egypt; it actually trampled down death by death. We mystical liturgists are marked with that same blood as a sphragis on our forehead. Every grave is an entrance to Hades; only one grave is its exit. It can be found outside the city walls of Jerusalem, but we can pass through its door at every liturgy. Christ's resurrected body could pass through

---

[10] Gregory the Great, *Moralia of Job*, vol. 3 (n.p.: Ex Fontibus, 2012), 258.

that stone as easily as it could later pass through the locked doors of the upper room, so the stone door was not rolled away to let him out, but to let the apostles see in. At every liturgy, we join Peter, the more fleet-footed John, Mary Magdalene, Joanna, Mary the mother of James, and all the other apostolic witnesses to stare again through this doorframe. It is the doorframe of the Church, which Gregory says has mystical (hidden) boundaries: "The Lord, coming to the Church in the flesh, measured out the measures of the earth with lines, because He marked out the boundaries of the Church with the subtlety of His secret judgment. . . . The lines of heavenly judgments were being stretched over the hidden spaces of the heart, in order that their incomprehensible measures might enclose the one within, and that the other might, not unjustly, remain without."[11] The liturgy that occurs within the hidden spaces of the heart is the liturgy hypostasized in the soul. *Liturgical asceticism* kneads both body and soul with that resurrection power; *liturgical mysticism* looks fixedly at the mystery, who is Christ risen; and *liturgical theology* illuminates our world and our place in it. Liturgical mysticism is the Trinitarian mystery, mediated by sacramental liturgy and hypostasized as personal liturgy, to anchor the substance of our lives.

---

[11] Gregory the Great, *Moralia of Job*, 3:255–256.

BIBLIOGRAPHY

Adam, Karl. *The Spirit of Catholicism*. New York: Angelico Press, 2012.

Aquinas, Thomas. *On Evil*. Notre Dame: University of Notre Dame Press, 1995.

Arintero, John. *The Mystical Evolution in the Development and Vitality of the Church*. 2 vols. Rockford, IL: Tan Books, 1978.

Aumann, Jordan. *Christian Spirituality in the Catholic Tradition*. San Francisco: Ignatius Press, 1985.

———. *Spiritual Theology*. New York: Bloomsbury Continuum, 2018.

Barsotti, Divo. *Il mistero Cristiano nell'anno liturgico*. Cinisello Balsamo, Italy: San Paolo Edizioni, 2006. In English *The Christian Mystery in the Liturgical Year*. Forthcoming.

———. *Suspended Between Two Abysses*. N.p.: Chorabooks, 2016. E-book.

Beauduin, Lambert. *Liturgy: The Life of the Church*. Farnborough, UK: Saint Michael's Abbey, 2002.

Behr, John. *Asceticism and Anthropology in Irenaeus and Clement*. Oxford: Oxford University Press, 2000.

Bernard of Clairvaux, *On the Song of Songs*. 4 vols. Kalamazoo, Michigan: Cistercian Publications, 1971.

———. *Selected Works*. New York: Paulist Press, 1987.

Bérulle. *Bérulle and the French School, Selected Writings*. New York: Paulist Press, 1989.

Bonaventure. *Holiness of Life*. London, UK: Catholic Way, 2013.

———. *Saint Bonaventure Collection*. Aeterna Press, 2016.

————. *The Soul's Journey into God, The Tree of Life, The Life of St. Francis.* Single Volume Edition. New York: Paulist Press, 1978.

Bouyer, Louis. *Christian Initiation.* New York: McMillan Company, 1960.

————. *Cosmos: the World and the Glory of God.* Petersham, MA: St. Bede's Publication, 1988.

————. *Introduction to the Spiritual Life.* Notre Dame, IN: Christian Classics, 2013.

————. *The Meaning of the Monastic Life.* London: Burnes & Oates, 1955.

————. *The Christian Mystery: From Pagan Myths to Christian Mysticism.* Edinburg: T&T Clark, 1990.

————. *The Church Of God: Body of Christ and Temple of the Spirit.* San Francisco: Ignatius Press, 2011.

————. *The Paschal Mystery: Meditations on the Last Three Days of Holy Week.* Chicago: Henry Regnery, 1950.

————. *The Seat of Wisdom: An Essay on the Place of the Virgin Mary and Christian Theology.* New York: Pantheon Books, 1960.

Cabasilas, *Nicholas. The Life in Christ.* Crestwood, NY: St. Vladimir's Seminary Press, 1974.

Cantalamessa, Raniero. *The Eucharist: Our Sanctification.* Collegeville, MN: Liturgical Press, 1995.

Catherine of Siena. *The Dialogue.* The Classics of Western Spirituality. New York: Paulist Press, 1980.

Chesterton, G. K. *Francis of Assisi.* In *G. K. Chesterton: Collected Works.* Vol. 2. San Francisco: Ignatius Press, 1986.

————. *Orthodoxy.* In *G.K. Chesterton Collected Works.* Vol. 1. San Francisco: Ignatius Press, 1986.

Claudel, Paul. *I Believe in God: A Meditation on the Apostles' Creed.* Edited by Agnes du Sarment. New York: Holt, Rinehart and Winston, 1963.

————. *Lord, Teach Us to Pray.* London: Dennis Dobson, 1942.

————. *The Essence of the Bible.* New York: Philosophical Library, 1957.

Clement of Alexandria, *The Stromata.* N.p.: Aeterna Press, 2016.

Clément, Olivier. *The Roots of Christian Mysticism.* Hyde Park, NY: New City Press, 1996.

Climacus, John. *Ladder of Divine Ascent.* New York: Paulist Press, 1982.

Code of Canon Law: A Text and Commentary, Study Edition. Commissioned by The Canon Law Society of America. Edited by James A. Coriden, Thomas J. Green, and Donald E. Heintschel. New York: Paulist Press, 1985.

Corbon, Jean. *The Wellspring of Worship.* San Francisco: Ignatius Press, 2005.

Daniélou, Jean. *Prayer: Mission of the Church.* Grand Rapids, MI: Eerdmans, 1996.

———. *The Bible and the Liturgy.* Notre Dame, IN: University of Notre Dame Press, 1966.

———. *The Lord of History.* New York: Longmans, Green & Co., 1958.

Davis, James Herbert, Jr. *Fénelon.* Boston: Twayne, 1979.

De la Bedoyre, Michael. *The Archbishop and the Lady.* New York: Pantheon Books, 1956.

De Sales, Francis. *Letters to Persons in Religion.* N.p.: Aeterna Press, 2015.

———. *Letters to Persons in the World.* N.p.: Aeterna Press, 2015.

———. *Treatise on the Love of God.* Blacksburg, VA: Wilder Publications, 2011.

Dionysius. *Pseudo-Dionysius: The Complete Works.* New York: Paulist Press, 1987.

Ephrem the Syrian. *Hymns on Paradise.* Crestwood, NY: Saint Vladimir's Seminary Press, 1990.

Escriva, Josemaria. *Christ Is Passing By.* New York: Scepter Press, 1990.

———. *Conversations with Josemaria Escriva.* New York: Scepter Press, 2002.

———. *The Way, Furrow, The Forge.* Single Volume Edition. New York: Scepter Publishers, 2011.

Evagrius. *The Praktikos & Chapters on Prayer.* Kalamazoo: Cistercian Publications, 1981.

Evdokimov, Paul. *Ages of the Spiritual Life.* Crestwood, NY: St. Vladimir's Press, 1998.

———. *The Art of the Icon: A Theology of Beauty.* Redondo Beach, CA: Oakwood, 1990.

Fagerberg, David. *Consecrating the World.* New York: Angelico Press, 2016.

———. *On Liturgical Asceticism.* Washington, DC: Catholic University of America Press, 2013.

———. *Theologia Prima: What Is Liturgical Theology?* Chicago: Hillenbrand Books, 2004.

Florensky, Pavel. *At the Crossroads of Science and Mysticism.* Kettering: OH, Semantron Press, an imprint of Angelico Press, 2014.

———. *The Pillar and Ground of the Truth.* Princeton: Princeton University Press, 1997.

François Fénelon. *Letters and Reflections of François Fénelon.* New York: World, 1955.

———. *Maxims of the Saints.* Atlanta, GA: Christian Books, 1984. www.ccel.org/ccel/fenelon/maxims/maxims.htm.

———. *Spiritual Letters of Archbishop Fénelon: Letters to Men.* London: Rivington's, 1927.

———. *Spiritual Letters of Archbishop Fénelon: Letters to Women.* London: Longmans, Green, & Co., 1900.

———. *Spiritual Progress.* New York: M. W. Dodd, 1853.

———. *The Seeking Heart.* Jacksonville, FL: SeedSowers, 1992.

Froget, Barthelemy. *The Indwelling of the Holy Spirit in the Souls of the Just According to the Teaching of St. Thomas Aquinas.* New York: Paulist Press, 1921.

Garrigou-Lagrange, Reginald. *Christian Perfection and Contemplation.* St. Louis, MO: B. Herder, 1945.

———. *Grace.* N.p.: Ex Fontibus, 2015.

———. *Reverend Reginald Garrigou-Lagrange O.P. Selection [5 Books].* N.p.: Aeterna Press, 2016.

———. *The Priest in Union with Christ.* Rockford, IL: Tan Books, 2002.

———. *The Three Ages of the Interior Life.* 2 vols. London: Catholic Weight, 2014.

———. *The Three Ways of the Spiritual Life: A Brief Outline of the Main Principles of Ascetical and Mystical Theology.* Rockford, IL: Tan Books, 1977.

Gillet, Lev. *Orthodox Spirituality.* Crestwood: St. Vladimir's Seminary Press, 1987.

Gilson, Etienne. *The Christian Philosophy of St. Thomas Aquinas.* Notre Dame: University of Notre Dame Press, 1956.

Gogol, Nikolai. *Meditations on the Divine Liturgy.* Jordanville, NY: Holy Trinity Monastery, 1985.

Gorday, Peter. *François Fénelon, a Biography.* Brewster, MA: Paraclete Press, 2012

Gregory of Nyssa. *From Glory to Glory: Texts from Gregory of Nyssa's Mystical Writings*. Compiled by Jean Daniélou. Crestwood, NY: St. Vladimir's Seminary Press, 1979.

Gregory the Great. *Moralia in Job*. 3 vols. N.p.: Ex Fontibus, 2012.

Gross, Jules. *The Divinization of the Christian According to the Greek Fathers*. Anaheim, CA: A&C Press, 2002.

Grou, Jean. *Manual for Interior Souls*. London: Burns, Oates & Washbourne, 1927.

Guyon, Jeanne. *Selected Writings*. New York: Paulist Press, 2012.

———. *Song of Songs*. Jacksonville, FL: SeedSowers, 2003.

———. *The Justifications*. 3 vols. Edited by Peter-John Parisis. Translated by Peter-John Parisis and Christopher P. Coty. Published by editor, 1992. https://www.akademijavjecnogproljeca.org/guyon/eng/The_Justifications_Guyon.pdf.

Heschel, Abraham. *The Sabbath*. New York: Farrar, Straus & Giroux, 1977.

Hierotheos, Metropolitan. *Hesychia and Theology: The Context for Man's Healing in the Orthodox Church*. Levadia, Greece: Birth of the Theotokos Monastery, 2007.

Holmer, Paul. "About Liturgy and Its Logic." *Worship* 50, no. 1. (January 1976): 18–28.

———. *C. S. Lewis: His Life and His Thought*. New York: Harper & Row, 1976.

Ignatius of Loyola. *The Autobiography of Saint Ignatius Loyola*. New York: Harper & Rowe, 1974.

Isaac the Syrian, *The Ascetical Homilies of Saint Isaac the Syrian*. Boston: Holy Transfiguration Monastery, 1984.

Isaiah of Scetis, *Ascetic Discourses*. Kalamazoo, MI: Cistercian Press, 2002.

John Damascene, *The Precious Pearl: The Lives of Saints Barlaam and Ioasaph*. Belmont, MA: Institute for Byzantine and Modern Greek Studies, 1997.

John of the Cross. *Ascent of Mount Carmel*. New York: Image Books, 1958.

———. *Dark Night of the Soul*. New York: Image Books, 1959.

———. *The Collected Works of St. John of the Cross*. Edited by Kieran Kavanaugh and Otilio Rodriguez. Washington, DC: Institute of Carmelite Studies, 1979.

John Paul II. Apostolic Letter *Novo Millennio Ineunte*. January 6, 2001. https://w2.vatican.va/content/john-paul-ii/en/apost_letters/2001/

documents/hf_jp-ii_apl_20010106_novo-millennio-ineunte.html.

Journet, Charles. *The Mass: The Presence of the Sacrifice of the Cross.* South Bend, IN: St. Augustine's Press, 2008.

Kavanagh, Aidan. *On Liturgical Theology.* New York: Pueblo Publishing, 1984.

Lallemant, Louis. *The Spiritual Doctrine of Father Louis Lallemant of the Society of Jesus.* Westminster, MD: Newman Press, 1955.

Lewis, C. S. *Screwtape Letters.* In *The Complete C. S. Lewis Signature Classics.* San Francisco: HarperSanFrancisco, 2007.

———. *The Pilgrim's Regress.* London: Fount Paperbacks, 1977.

———. *The Weight of Glory and Other Addresses.* New York: HarperOne, 2001.

Libermann, Francis. *Jesus Through Jewish Eyes: A Spiritual Commentary on the Gospel of St. John.* 3 vols. Blackrock, Co. Dublin: Paraclete Press, Blackrock College, 1995–2005.

———. *The Birth of Missionary Spirituality: Provisional Rule of the Missionaries of Libermann.* Deli, India: Facsimile, 2018.

———. *The Spiritual Letters of the Venerable Francis Libermann.* Vol. 1, "Letters to Religious Sisters and Aspirants." Duquesne Studies, Spiritan Series 5. Edited by Walter Van De Putte. Pittsburgh: Duquesne University Press, 1962.

———. *The Spiritual Letters of the Venerable Francis Libermann.* Vol. 2, "Letters to People in the World." Duquesne Studies, Spiritan Series 6. Edited by Walter Van De Putte. Pittsburgh: Duquesne University Press, 1963.

———. *The Spiritual Letters of the Venerable Francis Libermann.* Vol. 3, "Letters to Clergy and Religious." Duquesne Studies, Spiritan Series 7. Edited by Walter Van De Putte. Pittsburgh: Duquesne University Press, 1963.

———. *The Spiritual Letters of the Venerable Francis Libermann.* Vol. 4, "Letters to Clergy and Religious." Duquesne Studies, Spiritan Series 8. Edited by Walter Van De Putte. Pittsburgh: Duquesne University press, 1964.

———. *The Spiritual Letters of the Venerable Francis Libermann.* Vol. 5, "Letters to People in the World." Duquesne Studies, Spiritan Series 9. Edited by Walter Van De Putte. Pittsburgh: Duquesne University Press, 1966.

MacDonald, George. *Unspoken Sermons.* First, Second, and Third Series. Whitehorn, CA: Johannsen, 1999.

Marmion, Columba. *Christ in His Mysteries*. Bethesda, MD: Zaccheus Press, 2008.

———. *Christ: The Ideal of the Monk*. San Francisco: Ignatius Press, 2005.

———. *Christ: The Ideal of the Priest*. San Francisco: Ignatius Press, 2005.

———. *Life of the Soul*. Bethesda, MD: Zaccheus Press, 2005.

Maximus the Confessor. *Selected Writings*. New York: Paulist Press, 1985.

McGinn, Bernard, *The Essential Writings of Christian Mysticism*. New York: Modern Library, 2006.

Mersch, Emile. *The Whole Christ: The Historical Development of the Doctrine of the Mystical Body in Scripture and Tradition*. Translated by John R. Kelly. Milwaukee: Bruce, 1938.

Michel, Virgil, O.S.B. *The Liturgy of the Church, according to the Roman Rite*. New York: Macmillan, 1937.

Möhler, John Adam. *Symbolism: Exposition of the Doctrinal Differences Between Catholics and Protestants as Evidenced by Their Symbolical Writings*. New York: Crossroad, 1997.

———. *Mystery and Mysticism: A Symposium*. London: Blackfriars Publications, 1956.

Pascal, Blaise. *Pensées*. New York: E. P. Dutton, 1958.

Patmore, Coventry. *The Rod, the Root, and the Flower*. London: George Bell and Sons, 1895.

Paul VI. "Layman Should Be World's Perfect Citizen." General Audience, May 1, 1969. http://www.ewtn.com/library/PAPALDOC/P6LAYMAN.HTM.

Péguy, Charles. *The Portal of the Mystery of Hope*. Grand Rapids, MI: Eerdmans, 1996. 10–11.

Portillo, Alvaro del. *Faithful and Laity in the Church: The Bases of Their Juridical Status*. Montreal: Wilson & Lafleur, 2014.

Prestige, G. L. *God in Patristic Thought*. London: SPCK, 1985.

Rahner, Hugo. *Man at Play*. New York: Herder & Herder, 1972.

Ratzinger, Joseph. Address to Catechists and Religion Teachers. December 12, 2000. https://www.ewtn.com/new_evangelization/Ratzinger.htm.

———. *Eschatology: Death and Eternal Life*. Washington, DC: Catholic University of America Press, 1988.

———. *Pilgrim Fellowship of Faith*. San Francisco: Ignatius Press, 2005.

————. *Theology of the Liturgy*. Vol. 11 of *Collected Works*. San Francisco: Ignatius Press, 2014.

————. *The Spirit of the Liturgy*. San Francisco: Ignatius Press, 2000.

Saudreau, Auguste. *The Degrees of the Spiritual Life: A Method of Directing Souls According to Their Progress in Virtue*. 2 vols. London: Forgotten Books, 2012.

————. *The Life of Union with God, and the Means of Attaining It, According to the Great Masters of Spirituality*. N.p.: St. Pius Press, 2011.

————. *The Mystical State: Its Nature and Phases*. Whitefish, MT: Kessinger Reprints, 2011.

Scheeben, Matthias. *Mariology*. 2 vols. Ex Fontibus, 2010.

————. *Nature and Grace*. St. Louis: B. Herder, 1954.

————. *The Glories of Divine Grace*. Rockford, IL: TAN Books, 2001.

————. *The Mysteries of Christianity*. Chestnut Ridge, NY: Crossroad, 2008.

Schmemann, Alexander. *Church, World, Mission*. Crestwood, NY: Saint Vladimir's Seminary Press, 1979.

————. *For the Life of the World*. Crestwood, NY: St. Vladimir's Seminary Press, 1973.

————. *Liturgy and Tradition*. Edited by Thomas Fisch. Crestwood, NY: St. Vladimir's Seminary Press, 1990.

————. *Of Water and the Spirit*. Crestwood, NY: St. Vladimir's Seminary Press, 1974.

————. *The Eucharist*. Crestwood, NY: St. Vladimir's Seminary Press, 1987.

————. *The Journals of Father Alexander Schmemann*. Crestwood, NY: St. Vladimir's Seminary Press, 2000.

Solovyov, Vladimir. *Lectures on Godmanhood*. London: Dennis Dobson, 1948.

Stolz, Anselm. *The Doctrine of Spiritual Perfection*. New York: Crossroad, 2001.

Symeon the New Theologian. *Hymns of Divine Love*. Denville, NJ: Dimension Books, 1976.

Teresa of Avila. *The Way of Perfection*. Westminster: Newman Press, 1948.

Tognetti, Serafino. *Divo Barsotti: Priest, Mystic, Father*. London: St Pauls [*sic*], 2013.

Van Kaam, Adrian L. *A Light to the Gentiles: The Life Story of the Venerable Francis Libermann*. Milwaukee: Bruce, 1959.

Vonier, Anscar. *The Human Soul*. London: B. Herder, 1913.

Ward, Benedicta. *Sayings of the Desert Fathers.* New York: Penguin, 2003.

Wittgenstein, Ludwig. *Culture and Value.* Chicago: University of Chicago Press, 1980.

Yarnold, Edward, S.J. *The Awe-Inspiring Rites of Initiation: The Origins of the RCIA.* Collegeville: Liturgical Press, 1994.

Zaleski, Philip, and Carol Zaleski. *Prayer, A History.* New York: Houghton Mifflin, 2005.

INDEX

above-below, 35, 75, 78, 101-02, 106, 111, 113, 143, 148

Adam and Eve, 38, 47, 62, 63, 98, 104, 108, 116, 129

agape, 18, 24, 32, 47, 63, 82

anthropology, 44, 47, 64, 117

antinomy, 77, 127-31, 140

appetites, 2, 38, 64, 66, 101-02, 103, 104, 106, 110, 115

Arintero, John, xi, 41, 58

asceticism vii, x-xii 12-13, 19, 24-27, 36, 58, 62, 65-66, 71-72, 74-76, 79, 88-89, 101, 110-11, 113, 130

askesis, x, 12, 23, 89, 103

Augustine, 18-19, 53, 129

Auman, Jordan, xii, 24, 41

baptism, baptismal, x-xi, xiii, 2, 18-19, 26, 27, 32, 34, 37-38, 41-44, 47, 51-52, 56-58, 61, 82, 84, 99, 116, 118, 130, 136-37

baptismal font, x, 34, 37-38, 43,

Thomas Aquinas, 4, 48, 51, 64, 78, 88, 105, 109

transitory, 129-30, 142

transubstantiation, 76, 135,

Trinity, x-xi, xiii-xiv, 3, 4, 12, 16, 30, 32, 33, 34, 39, 40, 44, 48, 83, 113, 150, 120

viaticum, 115, 137-39

visible & invisible, xiii, 39-40, 46, 58, 65, 111, 118, 146,

von Rad, Gerhard, 45

Vonier, Anscar, 48

Wittgenstein, Ludwig, 7, 94

world, xii, xiv, 4, 6, 11, 14-15, 23, 25, 27, 29, 31, 35-37, 39, 43, 46-47, 51, 61-64, 68, 73-75, 77-78, 81-83, 90, 93-94, 96, 99, 101, 106-07, 110, 108, 111-13, 115-20, 127, 129-33, 135-41, 145, 148-49

worldliness, 73-74, 89, 106, 130, 131, 139